Leadership

It Takes More Than a Great Haircut!

Leadership

It Takes More Than a Great Haircut!

Terry L. Sumerlin

Leadership:
It Takes More Than a Great Haircut!

By Terry L. Sumerlin

©Terry L. Sumerlin, 2011

First Printing 2011
Printed in the United States of America

Cover Artist: Aundrea Hernandez

Published by:
SE Publishing
6338 N. New Braunfels #180
San Antonio, TX 78209

ISBN: 9780965966238

DEDICATION

I lovingly dedicate this book to Sherry, my practical realist, who for 41 years has loved and believed in this idealistic dreamer. She's kept my feet on the ground when my head was often in a book or in the clouds. She's my first and only sweetheart and I could not do what I do without her love and confidence in me.

ACKNOWLEDGEMENTS

In July, 2002 I began a wonderful relationship with *American City Business Journals*. It has provided not simply an outlet for my random thoughts, but a means of sharing my leadership message every month with tens of thousands of readers.

The carefully selected chapters in this book first appeared as columns in the *San Antonio Business Journal* (2002 – 2010). They are presented in the order of their appearance in the *Journal* in order to keep references to time intact. However, the book is not a diary or personal journal.

I am deeply indebted to Bill Conroy, editor, and Kent Krauss, publisher, of the *San Antonio Business Journal* for the relationship we have enjoyed and for permitting me to use these articles in this book. I'm honored to be a part of such a fine publication.

A SPECIAL THANK YOU to Laurie Magers for reviewing my manuscript and for her editorial suggestions. Because of her, this book is so much better. Her "master's in nice" makes her a very special person.

TABLE OF CONTENTS

FOREWORD

Terry Sumerlin does a marvelous job of translating life's daily occurrences in business into wonderful teaching moments on leadership. He possesses an uncanny wisdom in sharing relevant stories that each of us can readily identify with while drawing simple leadership applications for our understanding. I appreciate how Terry discusses the value of interpersonal skills when tact, respect and dignity are applied in a manner that does not compromise our values in the process. Leadership is about how well we influence, and Terry's work, *Leadership: It Takes More Than a Great Haircut!,* succeeds in demonstrating that leadership thrives in diverse, complex organizations as well as the most simplistic and unsophisticated of organizations. Terry validates that true leaders can lead in any business climate regardless of the circumstances and that, at the fundamental core, leadership is seeking out how to connect and understand those you lead by adding value to their lives.
  - Casey D. Blake, Major General, USAF

General Blake's views and opinions are his own and do not represent the United States Air Force.

PREFACE

Parents of grown children have many memories. Fortunately, for Sherry and me most of our memories are good.

One of my favorite memories is of a time we were dining out. Our son, Jon, was at the time in his early teens.

I paid for the meal with a credit card. So the cashier handed me a pen and the slip of paper for my signature.

My first book had just come out, and Jon was very proud of his author dad. With the book fresh on his mind, as I signed my name, Jon gave instructions to the cashier: "I would save that autograph if I were you. One of these days my dad is gonna be famous."

The lady looked at him like, "I guess." I was **speechless**—in more ways than one. What I mean is that back then I was often without a place to speak, which is not good for a professional speaker. So, my son's unconditional confidence in my success was a much needed boost to my ego.

At this point you might be expecting me to say that now, twelve years after *Barber-osophy – Shear Success for Your Cutting Edge*, Jon's prediction came true and I'm famous. However, I believe if you have to tell people you're famous, you're not!

But I'm not complaining. Rather, I'm thankful for so many wonderful opportunities. As a speaker and author, I've been privileged to travel to 25 states and 18 countries. Occasionally, I even see someone in the airport or while out and about who knows me from my work.

My face is not as recognizable, though, as is that of a few of my friends. But, at least, my picture isn't hanging on the wall in the post office. So, I guess my friends and I have that in common.

We have something else in common—an ongoing need to positively influence others. You have this need as well.

Regardless of who we are, where we are located or how we spend our time, with a positive influence we are able to make a lasting difference in the lives of others. Unlike management skills that focus on doing things right, this positive influence focuses on doing the right things. It's the essence of leadership.

This book focuses on this type of leadership in a very practical, common-sense manner. Both as the owner of a 54-year-old barbershop (called J.B.'s after my uncle who founded it) and as one who travels the world speaking as The Barber-osopher, I see innumerable examples every day of positive influence or a lack thereof.

As you read these illustrative anecdotes, you might frequently laugh. Since I wish to consider myself a humorist, I'd be disappointed if you didn't. More importantly, I hope that through the application of the principles illustrated by the anecdotes your positive influence will become even greater.

Always remember that leadership involves constant effort—and more than a great haircut!

A REAL BUILD UP

I cut a friend's hair for the first time. I was honored that he gave me his business, and so I spent a little extra time making sure he was pleased with the finished product.

Later that evening when I saw his wife I asked how she liked her husband's haircut. She said that she liked it, and then indicated that her husband also liked it. In fact, she added, "He said, `Terry's a perfectionist.'"

Believe me, I'm not a perfectionist. Sherry would tell you that I'm more the any-job-worth-doing-is-worth-doing-good-enough type. It leaves more time for reading good books. However, I know the type of tasks that deserve my very best effort, and my friend's haircut was always one of that type.

Compliments have that power of bringing out the best in people, and of giving the receiver a certain standard to live up to. They also cause a person to feel better about him or herself. Knowing this, Mark Twain said, "I can live two months on a good compliment."

In light of these observations, why do most of us not pay enough compliments? Why do many in business do the very opposite and find fault like there's a reward for it—or just say nothing at all when things are okay? It's probably more out of carelessness than it is by choice.

Such a practice reminds me of the 10-year-old boy who had never said a word. His parents spent tons of money on doctors, therapists, psychologists and what have you—all to no avail! Finally, one morning the little boy slammed his fist on the breakfast table and shouted, "This toast is burnt!" His mom and dad were astounded. They grabbed the child and hugged him tightly, while the tears flowed freely. Finally, they asked him why for all those years he had said nothing and then finally had decided to speak.

"Until now," he said, "everything's been okay."

Though we might chuckle at this story, try to imagine how it is to work for someone with such an approach. Maybe such doesn't greatly tax your imagination. Now ask yourself honestly, "Does this describe me?"

The answer to this question could contain the answer to some related questions. These could be questions like why we have low staff loyalty, why we experience heavy turnover, why productivity is low or why conflict is high. It could be because people feel unappreciated and unimportant.

Many monuments and great businesses have been built as testimonials to those leaders who knew how to show appreciation and how to make other people feel important. Aspire to that level of influence.

LEADERSHIP PRINCIPLE: Build lasting relationships and businesses by building up others.

J-O-B TYPE LEADERSHIP

"I ain't workin' here no more."

You may recognize these words from the Johnny Paycheck hit in which he spoke of telling his boss what he could do with his job. You may also recognize the attitude. Most feel that way from time to time, whether they own the business or work for someone else.

Though there is not much to be done for those whose mindset is to quit looking for work as soon as they find a job, what about the rest of us who from time to time feel like throwing in the towel? What are some of the causes and cures of the workin' man (or woman) blues?

First of all, understand that the problem generally has nothing to do with money. Many work for very little and are perfectly content, while others earn large incomes and are miserable. So, while a person might be unhappy on the job for lots of reasons, more money is rarely the solution.

Often the problem starts with a lack of appreciation. All can say that sometimes they feel used or taken for granted. Yet, it would be highly unusual for a worker to never, ever receive any appreciation. Maybe on those occasions when we do receive appreciation it would help if we placed written evidence of the compliment in an "appreciation folder," for future reference when the blues hit. That way we might avoid the no-one-ever-appreciates-anything-I-do syndrome.

Another possible solution is to occasionally ask ourselves what kind of appreciation we are looking for or expect. For instance, even though I occasionally get a standing ovation when I speak, should I expect an ovation after each haircut?

Maybe I should, rather, think in terms of how many repeat customers I have. Isn't that a form of appreciation? Actually, appreciation comes in lots of forms — both spoken and unspoken. Yet, however appreciation is given, if it isn't what we expect it to be, it might go unnoticed. Then we could get discouraged, or might eventually want to give up.

Another cause of burnout is futility. This is the feeling of not getting anywhere, or of having unattainable goals. In this case, it could be we need to set new goals or find better ways of reaching our existing ones. In the same way that we don't cancel our trip just because a given route is blocked, we shouldn't give up on achieving things that are really important to us because there is a flaw in our road map.

A third cause for giving up can be stress. This is like the story of the guy who was given the job of separating the big potatoes from the little ones. After a couple of weeks he wanted to quit. When asked if the work was more than he could handle he replied, "No, the work is not bad at all. It's just the decisions that are driving me nuts." It could be that some decisions could be handed off or shared, resulting in a lower stress level.

Also, some decisions can even be postponed until a better frame of mind prevails. In certain cases, Scarlet O'Hara's approach is best: "I'll worry about that tomorrow."

Lastly, when we speak of negative attitudes toward our careers, we need to include self-pity. Personally, I know that I'm too susceptible to pity parties. On such days, it's easy to feel sorry for myself because I feel trapped behind a barber chair, because I didn't get the speaking engagement I really wanted or because I'm just being silly. Poor me!

During such times, something Socrates said is especially meaningful. He said that if all the human suffering and hardship of all the ages were put into one huge pile, and each person then made to take an equal portion, most would be happy to just carry away the problems they brought to the pile.

It's something to think about.

If we're employed, I'm sure there are many who are unemployed who would gladly trade places with us. If our health permits us to go to work each day, again, there are those who would love to be in our places. In other words, think and thank!

LEADERSHIP PRINCIPLE: When your job gets you down, quickly find and use ways to get back up.

SIXTY SECONDS FOR TIME MANAGEMENT

Have you ever felt like you had too much to do, and too little time to do it? That's sort of like being asked if you've ever drawn a breath. Right?

Recently, I felt that way. With business, writing and home responsibilities, it all seemed a little overwhelming. What can we do at such times?

I readily admit not having all the answers. In fact, I turn down invitations to speak on time management simply because it's not my area of expertise. Nonetheless, there are a few techniques that help when I feel I'm drowning in "to do's." Maybe they will help you.

1. Keep some sort of "to do" list. Whatever it is you have to do, add it to the list. Oftentimes, just seeing a task, worry or problem in writing is enough to make it seem less daunting. Maybe it's because such a list reduces the opportunity for the imagination to work overtime on vagaries of the mind.

Also, once you've written down what you need to do: prioritize. Keep in mind that part of prioritizing is determining what is important, and what seems urgent. Sometimes, important things are urgent. However, not all urgent matters are important. Also, there are trivial things that, if left undone, are certainly not going to cause the world to come to an end. Yet, these are often the very things that **seem** important or urgent, and create the most stress.

2. Take a one-at-a-time approach. One of the most difficult things for me to remember about the barber business is that, whether the shop is full of customers or whether they come and go one at a time, I can only cut one head of hair at a time. On a

much larger scale, that's the way life works. We can effectively solve only one problem at a time. However, trying to do otherwise, we stress.

3. Delegate. How many times have we heard or read this? Yet, how often do we remember it? On the occasion I first mentioned, when I felt so overwhelmed, it suddenly dawned on me that I have a son who is much better equipped (physically and time-wise) to do some of the yard work that had piled up. Why hadn't I turned that over to him? Partly because I felt I was the only one who could do it like it ought to be done.

Sound familiar? What is there in your day that someone else could take care of, if only you would trust him/her with the task? When it comes to delegation, don't be someone who, so to speak, buys all the books on the subject and then simply chews on the covers. Take action!

4. Focus on goals more than tasks. That's not to say we can reach our goals while forgetting necessary tasks. However, it's easy to let tasks become goals, rather than means to goals. Put another way, life's objective is not to have an empty "in-basket." Actually, when we die, there will still be "stuff" in our "in-basket." But, that's okay. What's not okay is an empty basket **and** an empty, aimless life.

LEADERSHIP PRINCIPLE: Make time your friend by managing it wisely.

ENTHUSIASM RUNS RAMPANT

Not too long ago, I saw an interesting bank ad on a billboard just off Interstate 37, near the Alamodome. It read, "Enthusiasm runs rampant in bank lobbies."

My thoughts began to run rampant.

What I began thinking involved the popular concept of enthusiasm. So I began to visualize the bank president, the vice president, the loan officers and all the tellers running around wearing party hats and blowing on party favors, while throwing confetti everywhere. After all, they have enthusiasm at their bank!

However, we know that what I imagined is not enthusiasm at all. It's excitement. And, there's a difference in the two. A big difference!

This difference can be seen at a local high school football game. Enthusiasm is when players grind it out on every play, even when the body starts rebelling to the will. Excitement, however, comes when a team scores the winning touchdown. The band plays, the cheerleaders jump up and down and fans go wild. It's brief, it's intense and it's temporary.

Enthusiasm, on the other hand, lasts much longer because it's rooted in a cause or a belief system. Unlike excitement, it goes beyond the moment and springs from deep within the individual. Some have described it as a "fire in the belly."

However it's described, it is so vital to success and, yet, so rare that you wonder how so many businesses have survived without it. Others, recognizing the problem, have turned to solutions that have been less than satisfactory. Thus, we wonder what can be done to create enthusiasm.

Some think that the solution is possibly a weekend retreat where employees or managers go to some exotic place, and brainstorm to come up with a mission statement that can be prominently displayed (and then forgotten) when they get home.

However, though such weekends and mission statements can result in much that is good and profitable, they too often seem to be merely Band-Aids.

A less expensive and more effective solution might be to start at the top, with leaders who have a mission in their hearts and who are able to transfer that commitment to followers. Then the task becomes one of finding and nurturing good people who share the mission. These people, in turn, find it natural to demonstrate their enthusiasm.

For example, if our barbers actually believe they are providing an invaluable service to others, then such easily transfers into remembering customers' names, giving customers what they want, being kind and courteous and generally treating customers as truly special people. Then enthusiasm runs rampant at J.B.'s Barber Shop.

Yet, if barbers sense that, as the owner, I don't love my business or I don't believe in what we're doing, then the business has a real problem. And no amount of rah-rah or gimmickry will provide a solution.

LEADERSHIP PRINCIPLE: Remember that enthusiasm is an inside job that starts at the top.

NAME AND CLAIM RELATIONSHIPS

"Your Honor, I'd like to change my name."

"Change your name?" the judge replies. "And why is that?"

"Well, because people are always making fun of me," the gentleman explains.

"They make fun of you because of your name?" the judge asked. "What's your name?"

"John Stinks," the man answered.

"Well, I can certainly see why folks would make fun of you, with a name like that. But, what do you want to change your name to?" the judge inquired.

Without a moment's hesitation, the fellow replied, "Bill."

With few exceptions, most of us are not made fun of because of our names.

In fact, quite often the very opposite is true. Our name becomes the means of receiving a subtle compliment through someone remembering and using it in conversation.

I was reminded of how nice it is for those in business to remember one's name, when I spent a few days in Corpus Christi, Texas, during a speaking engagement. From the time I checked into the Omni Bayfront, I was "Mr. Sumerlin." It had a nice ring to it! It made me feel like a special guest of the hotel, and once again reminded me that there is no sweeter sound in any language than the sound of a person's own name. So, I determined to renew my efforts at remembering names.

If you experience the same challenges here as I do, maybe a few suggestions will help. They are common-sense ideas that have paid huge dividends for those who wish to build relationships.

There is a German proverb that says, "A poor memory has its roots in poor attention." Nowhere is this more apparent than with names. Oftentimes we don't forget a name. We never knew it to start with, simply because we weren't paying attention when the name was given. However, a person who is serious about remembering names makes sure to get the name during the introduction, even if it involves asking for it to be repeated or spelled.

Having gotten the name during the introduction, then we must immediately begin using it in conversation. "Well, Ms. Burns, how long have you been in San Antonio? How do you spend most of your time these days, Ms. Burns?"

This serves as a compliment to Ms. Burns, but also as a means of fixing the name in the mind. However, a note of caution: Don't overdo the use of the name. Once, while in a restaurant with my parents, the waitress was too obvious with our names. It became irritating to the point of sounding a lot like, "Can I get you anything else, Terry, before you leave me that huge tip?"

In addition to paying attention when we hear the name, and repeating it in conversation, there is one other technique we can use that helps with names: association. This involves some creativity and imagination. You might imagine your new acquaintance engaged in some activity (such as shaking hands) with another of your friends by the same name. Or you could picture the person doing something suggested by the name (Baker, Carpenter, etc.). The possibilities are endless. However, the more ridiculous the mental picture, the more likely we are to remember.

Yet, even if we apply all these techniques, and more, we still need to make allowances for occasional lapses in memory. Here, the words of a fictitious judge are appropriate. When the judge sentenced a 90-year-old man to 50 years, the man tried to reason with the judge by saying that he would not live long enough to serve out the sentence. The reply of the judge was, "Just get in there and do your best."

If we just do our best at remembering names, it might be an improvement over what we've been doing. And, it will certainly enhance relationships.

LEADERSHIP PRINCIPLE: To build relationships make it a point to call others by name.

HUMOR ME PLEASE

The little boy was nearly asleep as I cut his hair. However, he seemed to come around just a little when his mom said, "You're not going to sleep, are you?"

I figured I might startle him into staying awake. So, with a smile, I merely said, "I fell asleep in the barber chair once, and you see what happened to me."

It didn't take customers long to make the connection between what I'd said and my smooth head. Everyone laughed, and the little customer stayed awake.

Because such light moments cost so little and mean so much, I wonder why we tend to take our work and ourselves so seriously. Have we simply fallen into a mindset that has taken the fun out of business? If so, it could be affecting customer and staff relations. It could also be increasing stress, while reducing productivity. Maybe we need to be reminded of the incredible power of humor.

First of all, humor sells. One of the first things I was told when I got into the speaking business was, "You only use humor if you want to get paid." I tell groups that, with humor, I'm sort of like the cross-eyed javelin thrower. I don't set any records, but I do keep the crowd alert. Yet, there is more to it than alertness. Most people are more easily persuaded or motivated while laughing.

Another thing humor accomplishes is that it often deflects criticism. A reporter reminded President Reagan that he once said he would resign the presidency when his memory failed. Reagan replied, "When did I say that?" By the time the laughter had passed, the criticism had been forgotten.

Sometimes you can even head off criticism with humor. Occasionally, when I turn a customer around to look at his haircut in the mirror, I'll jokingly ask, "You think that'll hold you until you can find a barber?" It always gets a chuckle.

But, one of the greatest benefits of humor is stress relief. Surely nothing could be more stressful than having the president's life in your hands. Yet, we're told, as the team of surgeons was about to remove an assassin's bullet that was lodged one inch from his heart, President Reagan looked up and said, "I sure hope you're all Republicans."

"Mr. President," came the surgeon's reply, "today we're **all** Republicans."

Don't you think that at that point the doctors were in a little better frame of mind for their work?

It sort of makes you wonder why many businesspeople stay so uptight. It also makes you wonder how we expect to motivate others in a firings-will-continue-until-morale-improves atmosphere. Humor is less stressful and much more productive.

Yet, as with most things, there is a down side to humor in the workplace. If inappropriate, it can get a person into a lot of trouble. The right time, the right place and the right content must always be considered.

Motive must also be considered. If a person is seeking to be a wise guy or a walking joke book, he will eventually be avoided. If, on the other hand, one is able to think outside the box, or is able to see life standing on its head, that's the stuff humor is made of. Tell others. Likely, they'll enjoy telling someone else.

LEADERSHIP PRINCIPLE: Because the power of humor is no laughing matter, use it often.

A WAKE-UP CALL FOR PROFESSIONALISM

During the weekend between Christmas and New Year's, my wife and I went to Plano (near Dallas) to enjoy a belated family dinner hosted by our youngest daughter and her husband. Because of limited space in their apartment, Sherry and I decided to get a room at a nearby hotel.

One morning I went downstairs rather early, thinking I would get a cup of coffee and read a book. Off the lobby of the hotel is an offset, step-down with a beautiful fireplace. I figured what better place to drink my coffee and read.

However, when I stepped to the entrance and peered in, what I saw took me back a bit. On the couch, in front of the fireplace, a young man was stretched out—asleep!

I couldn't believe it. We weren't in some sort of cheap motel. It was an upper middle-class facility. I was dumbfounded.

Yet, not to be deterred, I walked over to the main lobby and sat in a comfortable chair, facing the registration desk. In a little while, I noticed a young man behind the desk. Sherry would have probably told me to keep reading my book. But, I couldn't resist.

"What is your occupancy this morning?" I asked.

"Huh?"

"How many vacant rooms do you have?"

"Oh. We're only about thirty percent," he replied.

"I see. Well, I was just wondering," I continued, "why, if you have plenty of rooms, a guest would be sleeping on the couch in front of the fireplace."

For a moment, he looked puzzled, and then he replied rather sheepishly, "Oh, that was me. I was just resting."

It was one of the few times I really didn't know what to say. I quickly went back to my book, and he went back to whatever he'd been doing—after his nap. However, since the incident, the topic of "professional standards" keeps rattling around in my head. We can be sure the hotel chain has them. In fact, most businesses have certain written or unwritten standards. Sometimes, these marks of professionalism are hardly detectable by the customer, yet recognized by insiders. Cumulatively, these "little things" make a powerful statement to the public. Consider several illustrations of such.

In the barbershop, one of the things I was taught very early is that barber chairs are for customers. They are not for barbers to lounge in. If a barber wants to sit, he should sit in a waiting chair.

Emergency medical services also have certain professional standards. I remember that some years ago, while being trained as an emergency care attendant for volunteer work in a small town, I heard the instructor say, "Don't run to an accident scene. Walk fast, but don't run. It only creates an atmosphere of panic and is not conducive to a clear head." Though the point might be debatable, it nonetheless stresses professionalism.

The third illustration involves the cultural shock of a certain young man, when he took a job at a local country club. He was told, "This country club requires collared shirts, especially of employees." Because he really wanted the job, our son went from T-shirts to collared shirts.

You might be wondering what all of this has to do with you as a leader. Actually, it involves two things: (1) the little marks of professionalism that set you apart from the rest, (2) and whether or not you enforce these policies.

I'm sure if you asked the hotel chain where we were staying how they felt about employees sleeping in the lobby, they would think you had dropped in from Mars. "Why would you ask such a question?" Yet, our question would be, "Why would you have standards you don't enforce?"

LEADERSHIP PRINCIPLE: Pay attention to the little things that say a lot about professionalism.

THE ONE YOU'RE ALWAYS WITH

About twenty years ago, I placed a call to a lady in Los Angeles who was in charge of passenger services for a cruise line. I told her I was seeking information about doing on-board motivational lectures for her passengers. She recommended I send her a packet of information, and she later added my name to her list of enrichment lecturers.

Thus began an incredible adventure in cruising. Yet, though my arrangement with cruise lines has provided the obvious, an opportunity to see the world, it has also been a means of observing people.

Actually, more people than ever are cruising. Because the industry offers more staterooms than there is demand, and because overall travel is down, cruise lines are offering incredible deals. So, cruises have become popular to a larger segment of the population.

Unfortunately, though, there are those who have been less than satisfied with the cruise experience, or who have simply been disappointed. There are many causes for such. However, there are a couple of causes that never show up on the comment questionnaire, but nonetheless have a negative impact on the overall experience. They are, by the way, the same factors that have a bearing on all of life's experiences. They are attitudinal.

So, whether you are planning a cruise or a life, maybe the following thoughts will be a source of "enrichment." And, for now, you don't even have to pack.

First of all, the problem many have on cruises is that they have to take themselves along. It's sort of like the old expression, "Wherever you go, there **you** are." So, many soon discover that they're not any happier in the lap of luxury, being waited on hand and foot, than they were at home waiting on themselves. This, I think, comes as a surprise!

We tend to think that the only thing necessary for happiness is a change in circumstance or environment. It's sort of like the teenage boy who left home, in a miserable state of mind. Before he left, his dad gave him a letter to be read when he got where he was going. One day as the boy sat on the beach, watching the waves and the surf, he opened the letter to see what Dad had to say. The letter simply said, "Well, son, you left in search of happiness that you couldn't find at home. But, no doubt, you're still unhappy, because you took with you the one person most responsible for your misery: yourself. When you realize this, come back home. Love, Mom and Dad."

I jokingly tell folks that, on the cruises I do, the average age of the passengers is deceased. Of a few of them, I've often thought it must be terrible to be old, rich, cranky and miserable. Yet, at some point they were probably young and miserable. Then they just got used to it. They could be miserable at home — and save their money.

The second thing I would mention is that cruises are not for everyone. In conversation with the CEO of an international cruise/travel agency, he made the statement that he is continually telling his salespeople that some people need to vacation somewhere besides on a cruise. He said just because fares are low doesn't mean a particular person would enjoy a cruise or can afford it. In fact, he said a least half the folks that go on cruises can't really afford them. So, there is no way to meet their expectations. They will have buyer's regret and bad feelings toward the agency.

Some of this type must have been among those I once saw in the gangway, literally booing an assistant cruise director because disembarkation was not going to their satisfaction. After all, they paid good money for that trip and deserved better treatment.

The problem was not with the cruise line or the young director. The problem was that expectations exceeded reality. What was expected was perfection. What they got was what we usually get from life—imperfection.

LEADERSHIP PRINCIPLE: Realize that life is life no matter where we go or what the trip cost.

HOW TO INSURE DEPOSITS

Behind my barber chair is a small, hinged door, covering what was once a bin for soiled towels. It is no longer used for that purpose, but rather, as a drop for change that is collected throughout the week. It has become a type of account, into which regular deposits are made prior to taking the money to the bank across the street.

These deposits are never very significant. However, there is another type of deposit that is most significant, into which I make frequent deposits. These deposits go into a trust account with customers and staff.

From both the small change account and the trust account there can be withdrawals. However, there is a difference in the nature of the withdrawals. In the case of the monetary account, when money that is withdrawn is put back, the account returns to its former balance. With a trust account, depending on the nature of the withdrawal, it may take numerous deposits to again gain someone's confidence. In fact, with certain words or actions one can get permanently overdrawn.

Such was apparently the case with a lady I heard about while speaking in Las Vegas. According to her employer, she was part of his staff that he had taken to Las Vegas. She came to him asking that he buy her a plane ticket home.

"I don't understand," he said. "Didn't you have a round trip ticket?"

It was then she confided she'd gotten cash on her return flight, had gambled that away and had also lost $10,000 on her credit cards. She was considerably in the red! Assuming she had a spouse back home, and that he found out what happened, I would guess she was "big time" in the red in her trust account.

Similarly, in our own trust accounts we make withdrawals and deposits of all types and sizes, and with varying rewards or consequences. Let's take a look at a few ways to make deposits with customers and employees.

One of the best deposits into our trust account is a positive attitude. It seems people are naturally attracted to, and have confidence in optimistic, positive, upbeat individuals. Not many want to be around someone who acts like she was weaned on a dill pickle. Most would much rather be around someone who looks like she ate a banana sideways.

Folks also want to do business with and follow those with integrity. Back when roofs lacked the quality they have now, and when people set out tubs to catch rainwater that dripped through the roof, an expression developed. To describe a person of integrity, one would say, "If he tells you it's gonna rain, you can set the tubs out. It's gonna rain." Businesses today need such people, who will do what they say they will do, when they say they will do it and in the manner they say they will do it. Unfortunately, lacking in this sort of integrity, many are overdrawn in their trust accounts.

Another way to make deposits with others is through kind words of encouragement. Encouragement is so universally needed. Yet, in spite of such, many make continued withdrawals from their accounts through criticizing others. Then they wonder why they lose their followers.

LEADERSHIP PRINCIPLE: Always strive to build a huge trust account through encouragement, integrity and a positive attitude

SOMETHING WORTH CATCHING

Abraham Lincoln said, "Most people are about as happy as they make up their minds to be." If that's true, and it seems that it is, then we see people every day who apparently have never made up their minds to be happy.

At J.B.'s Barber Shop we see two contrasting types of individuals. We see the type that has a spring in his step, and song in his heart and a gleam in his eye. This person brightens a room just by entering. Then, conversely, once in a while we see the kind of fellow who, if portrayed in a cartoon, would have a dark cloud over his head. This person just exudes doom, gloom and cynicism. This person brightens a room too—just by leaving!

What might be the reason for this difference in personalities? Surely it's not preplanned. I have yet to have someone tell me: "Terry, before you start cutting my hair, there's something I need to tell you. This morning I suddenly realized I haven't been unhappy in a whole month. And, I sure don't want to lose my unhappy side. So, I decided that today I would practice being unhappy."

I've never run across anyone that demented. Yet, occasionally I encounter an unhappy person. So, if as Lincoln says most people are about as happy as they make up their minds to be, and if it's not preplanned, it must nonetheless be by choice.

Before looking at such choices, let's briefly look at the "so what" of happiness. What if a person is unhappy? Does attitude matter? So what?

Part of dealing with the "so what" involves a simple question: If you're habitually unhappy, how's that working for you? Additionally, the importance of a proper attitude can be seen in how it affects those around us, both on and off the job. Attitude is contagious. We want an attitude that's worth catching.

With these things in mind, let's look at two choices we make, having to do with ourselves, and how these choices in perception affect our happiness.

The first choice has to do with our appearance. As I think of this, I'm reminded of a beautiful, intelligent young lady that once worked for a business I frequent. I remember that she once had beautiful blond hair. Then one day I was startled to see that she had become a decided redhead. That is, she just decided to be a redhead.

She was still beautiful. Yet I couldn't help thinking that if there was something about the appearance of such an attractive young lady that she, herself, didn't like; what about the rest of us? Who does not sometimes feel he/she is too tall, too short, too thin, too fluffy or too something? Within reason, some things can be changed or improved upon. Yet, at some point, we have to accept the fact that, though we have bodies, we are not our bodies. Or, we have hair (sometimes), but we are not our hair. It's an attitudinal choice that can greatly affect our happiness.

Similarly, how we feel about what we do can influence our attitude. Believe it or not, at one time I was reluctant to tell others I'm a barber. The occupation didn't seem prestigious enough. Then, I realized the job doesn't give dignity. We give dignity to the job. Furthermore, we are not what we do, any more than we are our bodies. We have bodies and we have jobs. But, we are greater than both.

LEADERSHIP PRINCIPLE: Choose to have an attitude worth catching.

WHEN GECKOS DO THE BACKSTROKE

I had just sat down and was about to open my book when the waitress brought my coffee. As she went back to the kitchen, I reached for the cup. However, just before taking my first sip, I noticed a foreign object floating in the coffee.

You've got to be kidding, I thought. That's surely not what I think it is. Sure enough, when I lifted the object with my fork and got a closer look, it was definitely what I thought it was—a dead gecko!

After collecting my thoughts, I took the cup and everything in it back to the kitchen. I decided against asking the waitress what a lizard was doing in my coffee, for fear of receiving the old line about the backstroke. Instead I simply informed her of the problem and then went back to my table.

In no time at all, the waitress, the hostess and the assistant manager, individually, came to my table to express their embarrassment and to apologize. Then a few days later, when I was back in the restaurant, the general manager made it a point to apologize and to say that such was an inexcusable oversight.

There was never an attempt to cover up or to offer excuses for what had happened. Apologies were profuse and sincere. And, as a result of the way the situation was handled, I will continue to frequent the restaurant and will have no fear of another occurrence. The incident reminds us, though, of something from which all in business can benefit: the proper way to deal with a customer crisis.

First and foremost is that we see the situation from the customer's point of view. In the same way that the difference in major and minor surgery is that major surgery is when it's mine, any problem a customer has should be considered major. It should never be treated lightly.

I'm reminded of the time my wife, Sherry, was burned by hot coffee while in a fast food restaurant. None of the employees, including a manager, seemed concerned. When I tried to get their attention, I was basically ignored. Their nonchalant attitude could have easily created a lawsuit, and when I later called the corporate office, I told them so. Conversely, we don't generally sue people we like and who manifest a caring attitude.

There is no escaping the fact we must truly care about those we serve. First of all, it's the right thing to do; secondly, it's good business.

The second thing we need to consider regarding the "gecko incident" is not only that we must care, but also that we should go out of our way to apologize (without excuse) and to make the situation right, if at all possible. We can't change what happened. The gecko was there! However, we can assure the customer we'll take steps to see that it never happens again. And, then, we must follow through.

Accept that things go wrong in business. Count on it. The question is: What then?

LEADERSHIP PRINCIPLE: In your business or place of employment, when bad things happen to good people quickly and compassionately right the wrong.

JOIN THE OPTIMIST CLUB

I'm an optimist. In fact, we're so optimistic in our home we have snooze buttons on our smoke alarms.

You've probably heard of the guy that walked up to a little league game and noticed on the scoreboard that one team was down 40-0. He commented to a player on the losing team, "You guys are taking quite a whipping today."

Without so much as batting an eye, the boy responded, "Yeah, but wait until we get to bat." In business, I'm that kind of optimist.

Yet, I realize that for some optimism seems corny and dumb. And, they may have good reason for feeling that way. It could be they've read or heard things about optimism that aren't so.

One of the impressions often left is that optimism is about all that is required to accomplish most anything. Such is misleading and ultimately disillusioning.

A more realistic view might be to recognize that, though optimism doesn't of itself equip a person to do anything, it does give a person the mindset to do what one has the skill to do—better than pessimism.

For instance, optimism alone won't make a person a surgeon. However, we certainly want a qualified surgeon with a can-do-attitude. Few things could be more disturbing than to have a competent surgeon stand over you and say, "This ain't gonna work."

Similarly, in business, skilled, knowledgeable and optimistic leaders are desired and needed. They are the ones who generally get greater productivity from their followers.

They also have less job related stress and experience less conflict.

Unfortunately, in some businesses, not only is the leader lacking in optimism, she discourages it on the part of others. Michael de St. Pierre addressed this problem when he said: "It may be true that an optimist sees a light where there is none, but why must a pessimist always run to blow it out?"

It is self-defeating for a leader to take this approach. So we wonder what would cause such. What's the cure? On this, I'll simply say one thing.

It could be that our fascination with the media is one of the major causes. Understand, this is not a criticism of the media per se. It has a legitimate role. However, news can give us a distorted, negative view of the whole world. This is due to the fact that unless something is the exception, it's generally not news. And, those things that are the exception are often negative. Recognizing and acting on this alone might improve our perspective.

LEADERSHIP PRINCIPLE: Beware of news that destroys healthy optimism.

SAY IT WITH CONFIDENCE

Recently, I was asked to serve as a personal coach to two individuals who want to develop their public speaking skills. My reaction was somewhat like the fellow who watched his mother-in-law drive off a cliff in his new BMW. I had mixed feelings.

I was honored by the request. Yet, it was somewhat humbling, since I don't consider myself an authority on public speaking. But, I'm willing to do what I can to help the two gentlemen.

Along this line, it seems that the business world is constantly making more demands for presentation skills; and, as a result, more men and women are looking for practical public speaking tips. Here are a few tips that have worked for me:

1. Know and love your subject. It would be nearly impossible to speak effectively on a subject one cares little about; and absolutely impossible to draw information out of an empty well.

Most speakers could illustrate the "knowing and loving" principle by reference to the various groups they are called on to address. In other words, I speak to many groups whose specific area of expertise or service is foreign to me. And, it would be foolish of me, in such cases, to pretend to be an industry expert. However, what I do understand through research, observation and experience (and what I have a passion for), are leadership and team building as they relate to various professions.

Similarly, there are things that you know—and know well. There are things you also believe in very strongly. These are the topics on which you might speak effectively.

2. Organize your thoughts. Regardless of how passionate you are or how well you know your subject, you must present it in an organized manner or it will fall on deaf ears. This is a weakness of many beginning speakers. And, although visual aids can help with this, they are no guarantee of organization. I recently heard a presenter who used PowerPoint, and the presentation had the organization of a flatcar full of scrap iron.

Some suggestions for improving speech organization might be to learn and use proper outlining techniques, record the presentation at home or in the office and then listen for flow and continuity, or practice on a friend and then ask for feedback.

Remember, audiences should never ask themselves, "Where is he now?" Let them clearly know what the points of the presentation are, and also when you are going from one thought to the next. Otherwise, they grow weary of trying to figure it out and then quit listening.

3. Get to the point. Abraham Lincoln once spoke of a political opponent as having the ability to compress the greatest number of words into the smallest thoughts. Not only do such speakers tend to go overtime (never a good practice), they tend to put an audience to sleep. Effective speakers work hard at finding the shortest distance between their thoughts and the listener's heart.

4. Use good illustrations. This column alone contains four illustrations. Good illustrations tend to keep a reader or audience alert, while serving to drive home a point. Because of such, we should use them freely. However, they need to always be in good taste. They should also have relevance, and be stories that we can relate comfortably.

5. Have fun. I've been told that Alben W. Barkley, vice president of the United States, is on a very short list of all those who have ever died while giving a speech. It's a fairly safe thing

to do. Simply pick out a few smiling faces scattered over the room, and speak to them. Next thing you know, you might enjoy the occasion in spite of yourself.

LEADERSHIP PRINCIPLE: Develop the ability to speak effectively in public.

DON'T GET CHEESY

One of the many stories President Reagan told involved communist Russia. He said that one of its citizens was finally able to save enough money to buy an automobile. So, he went to the proper bureau and filled out all the necessary papers for his purchase. Having done that, he was given a date of delivery that was five years away.

"Will that delivery be for the morning or afternoon?" the man asked.

The agent shot back, "What difference does it make? We're talking about something five years away?"

"Because," the gentleman replied, "the plumber's already scheduled for that morning."

Reagan would use the illustration to point out the inefficiency of Russia's whole system. He would also, quite often, say that the number one job of a bureaucracy is to preserve the bureaucracy.

All of this came to mind when I was called on to give a speech to a governmental agency. I was specifically asked to deal with how to motivate those who are constantly coping with regulations and red tape. Though a challenge to agencies, it's also the challenge of many in the private sector.

Fortunately, at J.B.'s Barber Shop we don't see a lot of bureaucratic red tape. However, we do answer to various agencies, including the Internal Revenue Service. And, the same is true of all businesses. None are unaffected. So how can we best cope?

First of all, since we have little choice, we can comply. However, in the process of complying we must also keep our priorities straight.

One of the things I tried to stress in the speech that I mentioned is that people are rarely highly motivated to serve bureaucracies. On the other hand, employees might have a better attitude toward tedious, boring or stressful procedures if leaders impress on them that they're performing tasks required by certain agencies, without which the business is not allowed to exist. And, by existing businesses provide the public with valuable services, products and jobs.

Looking at the matter from the customer's point of view, there is something else we can do in the midst of bureaucratic procedures: We can shield him from as much of it as possible, and thus make it easier to do business with us.

An example of failure to take care of the customer in this way involves something that happened years ago in a hotel restaurant. I ordered a cheese Danish and received this reply from the waitress: "I'll see if we have one. Normally management doesn't like us to tell customers when we have them, because when we tell them we sell out too fast."

I thought I was hearing things, or had just been beamed down from the Starship Enterprise. But, it got even stranger.

The dear lady then went off in search of my priceless pastry, and in a few minutes came back to the table carrying my Danish on a saucer as if she bore the Hope Diamond. She had performed for me this grand service.

I still laugh every time I relate the ridiculous scenario in speeches. Yet, the sad part is that to management and employees of the restaurant the rationale behind their approach probably made perfect sense. The absurdity of it all, and how it epitomized slavery to a ridiculous system, was apparent only to certain guests.

The incident, itself, didn't involve regulations from some sort of governmental agency. However, it nonetheless illustrates an approach taken by many businesses. It involves, above all things, strict adherence to systems, policies and ordering procedures rather than attention to serving the public and making a profit. As a result, the customer tends to lose patience in trying to do business, and the business tends to lose customers.

At J.B.'s Barber Shop, customers don't need or want an explanation of barber codes and standards before they're allowed to get in the barber chair. They just want customer oriented service that gets them in and out. It's probably the same way in your business.

LEADERSHIP PRINCIPLE: Whatever rules, regulations and systems are used in your business, keep them subordinate to people and profit.

'NO FURTHER ADIEU' WON'T DO

When I first began trying to become a professional speaker, I did what many have done. I spoke for free to anyone who would have me. Along with other types of groups, this involved a lot of civic organizations. These groups provide wonderful community service, and provide lots of beginning speakers with needed experience. They can also **be** an experience.

I recall a certain early morning presentation to just such a group. We had our breakfast, and it was time for the program. The fellow who was supposed to introduce me stepped to the mic, sort of cleared his throat and stammered around a bit. Then he suddenly said, "Oh, I almost forgot! Let's go ahead and have our drawing for the door prize before we have our speaker." When that matter was disposed of, he turned to me and said, "Now we'll have our speaker." That was it! That was how I was presented to the group and how they were warmed up for me.

Conversely, I spoke to a San Antonio group, where I was preceded at the microphone by then Councilman Carroll Schubert. Though he was not the one officially designated to introduce me, he endeared himself to me when he said he regularly read my "barber-osophy column" and that the audience was in for a treat.

Obviously, one introduction was of great service to the group and to me. The other was as useful as a sidesaddle on a sow. Since many find themselves in the role of introducing a speaker to groups of various types and sizes, maybe the following suggestions will help:

1. Prepare. Do not try to wing it. Have the speaker give you a biography well in advance of the meeting, and then use it.

Though you don't have to read it—however, if done well that is acceptable—don't stray too far from it.

2. Organize your material. A simple, straightforward approach is often best. Some prefer the T-I-S formula—the topic, its importance and relevance, and then the speaker's background and qualifications. The last words spoken should be the speaker's name, spoken clearly and to the audience. Turn toward the audience, not toward the speaker who already knows her own name, and say something like, "With pleasure, I present_____."

3. Warm up the audience. This is the vital purpose of an introduction. So, be conversational, personable and engaging. Then, lead the applause, as the speaker makes his way to the platform!

4. Keep it brief. Somewhat like a good haircut, it should be long enough to cover the subject, yet short enough to please. The introduction is not the main event, and it's most impressive when its purpose is not to impress.

5. Be careful with humor. Sometimes humor in introductions is at the expense of someone in the audience, the speaker or the speaker's allotted time. Again, preparation here is the key. Winging it on humor has often caused embarrassment to someone, or created unnecessarily long-winded stories at the mic. Quips or one-liners are often best. However, if you must tell a rather long story (that you're sure 75 percent of the crowd hasn't already heard), remember this: The longer the story, the stronger the punch line better be. Otherwise, listeners feel cheated.

6. Create reasonable expectations. For example, a humorist doesn't want to be introduced as the funniest person alive. In fact, superlatives should be used sparingly. Let the speaker's presentation speak for itself.

LEADERSHIP PRINCIPLE: A speaker introduction is a way of rendering a valuable service while showing class.

LOOK OUT FOR BISCUITS AND TERMITES

I happen to like McDonald's coffee. So, whether at home or traveling, I usually get my daily quota. In the process, I see things that arrest my attention.

For instance, in the restaurant not too far from our home, in the mornings my wife and I are often greeted by friendly ladies—who proudly have our coffee and Sherry's yogurt parfait on the tray by the time we get to the serving counter. It's a little thing that makes a big impression.

In Honolulu, I noticed an interesting indication of the Hawaiian culture at their McDonald's. For breakfast they serve scrambled eggs with Spam and rice.

One of the most unusual sights I've encountered was a sign in a McDonald's in the Minneapolis-St. Paul Airport. It said, "This McDonald's does not serve biscuits." I did a double take. What? It seemed almost un-American.

Looking back on the situation, and having had time to do some analyzing, what I concluded was this: Since I was there about a month after 9-11, it must have been that the McDonald's people received credible information that there was the threat of a hijacking at that airport, in which McDonald's biscuits would be hurled at passengers. Thus, their decision.

That's the way I reasoned, while thinking from a fearful, weird point of view. But, when reason prevailed, so did a more rational explanation. Likely, the "Spam in Hawaii," and the "no biscuits" in Minneapolis were simple business decisions. Nothing more or less.

All of this came to mind, following a recent conversation with my next door neighbor. He somewhat excitedly asked, "You got any termites in your house?"

"Not that I know of," I replied.

"Well, I wanted to let you know," he said. "My wife saw some in one of our bathrooms, and I'm gonna get me an exterminator. I want him to drill holes in the foundation and give us the full treatment. It's expensive, but I don't want those things to get started."

A couple of days later, he caught me as I was pulling out of our driveway. He was laughing, as he said, "We found out we don't have termites. The exterminator said those are ants."

Now, before we shake our heads too much at my neighbor or at my biscuit story, let's ask ourselves a few questions. If we were to get an unexpected letter tomorrow from the IRS, would we immediately think that it's bad news, or would we think maybe it's a refund?

If the phone rings in the middle of the night, how often do we think it's a wrong number? Got to be bad news, right? Other such illustrations could be given. But, the point is that this fear often replaces rational thinking. And, we are daily bombarded with stuff that can make us afraid.

My neighbor is a reasonable and intelligent person. However, that does not keep him from being susceptible to "fear-based advertising."

Likely, in his mind, the inclination to think the worst had conjured up images of insects that could level a redwood forest in less than 30 minutes. And, since fear of loss is generally stronger than desire for gain, he was primed to hand over his money.

In that respect, we are all susceptible to fear-based advertising—whether through news reports, FYI type programming, word of mouth or other means. We are often covered with negative, fear inducing (mis)information. And, since the most exercise many of us get is in jumping to wrong conclusions, we become more and more anxious.

Therefore, as consumers, some tend to miss out on wise purchases and good investments because they see everything as scams and everyone as shysters. Viewed from another perspective, business people who are affected by such negative input often become cynical, negative, and reactionary; thus repelling customers and stifling their own enthusiasm and creativity.

It seems there are times when we need to imitate the approach of the smoker who, many years ago, read the latest medical reports on the health risks of smoking. When asked what he decided, he replied, "I've decided to quit reading that stuff!" Though his decision was foolhardy, a similar approach with respect to certain negative input might be the better part of wisdom.

LEADERSHIP PRINCIPLE: To avoid knee-jerk business and personal conclusions or decisions, beware of (mis)information based on fear.

LISTEN UP

With some things, there is an expected and natural response. For instance, if you toss something in another's direction, you're not surprised when the person reaches out to catch it. Similarly, when we smile others usually smile back. What about when we speak or when someone speaks to us? It seems that listening would be the natural response. Too often, it's not.

That doesn't mean that we fail to look at the speaker or to receive sounds. We might even give appropriate responses. However, effective listening demands so much more of us. Let's look at those demands.

First of all, effective listening demands undivided attention. Many years ago, I worked for a barber who would get so engrossed in what he was telling a customer that he would shut off his clippers, stop working and stand in front of his customer. There he would hold court. I wonder how a customer would feel if I turned off my clippers and did the same thing just to listen to him. You might also ask yourself the same type of question with respect to your customers, employees, spouse, children and friends. Not only is such treatment a high compliment. Undivided attention greatly reduces misunderstandings. Wandering eyes and busyness, on the other hand, are insulting and constitute ineffective listening.

Secondly, let's think about listening in relation to proper use of the eyes. Studies have shown that confident people tend to look others in the eye for approximately seven seconds and then look away for about seven seconds before looking back. Looking away, however, doesn't mean a distracted type of looking about. Nor should we be looking at people as if to bore a hole through them. We should be looking as a means of listening. The eyes tell us many things that the ears do not. The ears don't pick up body language, gestures, facial expressions and overall demeanor. Yet, they all affect meaning.

The third factor affecting how well we listen is the condition of the mind. Our auditory system doesn't work properly if there is a short circuit in the brain. Similarly, if our minds are not open we don't listen well. The result can be what our spouses sometimes call selective listening. As an illustration, I hear baseball announcers on TV just fine. I tend not to hear Sherry very well, though, when she tells me something during a game. I also don't hear very well when I've already made up my mind on the matter.

Most importantly, though, effective listening involves the heart. This reminds me of one of my favorite people, Art Linkletter. He was such a great listener. I fondly remember, as a child, watching his House Party and hearing his wonderful interviews with children.

One day, Art had an especially interesting conversation with a little boy. The conversation went somewhat in this manner:

"What is your name?" Art asked.

"Tommy."

"How old are you, Tommy?

"Eight."

"What do you want to be when you grow up?"

"I want to be an airplane pilot," Tommy replied.

"Wow, that's great! Would you like to pretend right now you're an airplane pilot, Tommy?"

The boy smiled and nodded in approval.

Art then said, "Okay. Let's pretend that you're flying a plane with two hundred passengers, across the ocean, and suddenly realize your engines are no longer working. What would you do?"

After thinking for a moment, Tommy replied, "First, I would put on the fasten seat belt sign. Then I would parachute out."

The studio audience roared with laughter. But, Art never took his eyes off the little boy. When the laughter ended, Art looked into the tear-streaked face of the little boy and asked,

"Tommy, why would you parachute out?"

"To go get fuel, of course."

Art got the rest of the story because he listened not just with his ears and eyes, but with his heart. That kind of listening will help us form better relationships both in and out of the workplace.

LEADERSHIP PRINCIPLE: Never confuse hearing sounds with effective listening.

HOW TO HANDLE DISAGREEMENT

If two people are together for any length of time they're going to disagree. It's not a matter of if. It's a matter of when. This should not surprise us.

Recently as a customer and I were talking about our different tastes in Mexican food, an 80-year-old customer came in with a picture of a 30-year-old male model. The model had beautiful jet black hair. Anticipating a "yes," the customer asked, "Terry, can you cut my hair like this picture?"

We disagreed as to whether that was possible.

These differences or disagreements are because we are different. Just as surely as we have different DNA, we have different tastes and draw different conclusions. And, when you add change to the mix, there are most definitely going to be some disagreements. Peter Shane, former Dean of the University of Pittsburgh Law School, said, "If you advocate change, you will have to understand that there is no change so small that it threatens no one."

Considering that we are all unique, and that we don't like change, we must learn to deal effectively and civilly with resultant disagreements—in our country, in the home and in the workplace. May I offer a few suggestions?

First of all, recognize that just because two people disagree doesn't necessarily mean something sinister is involved. You might disagree with me because you're my friend, and you're trying to help me in some way. Certainly disagreement might actually come from an enemy, just as someone who's paranoid might really have someone after him. But, why must we assume it is always an enemy who disagrees? Such an assumption tends to reveal immaturity and insecurity.

Secondly, when discussing a disagreement there are several things we might want to keep in mind.

1. Be sure to clearly understand what the other person is saying. Unless you are able to state the other person's position in such a way that he/she would say "that is absolutely correct," there is no legitimate basis for disagreement. In fact, it could be that when the matter is properly understood everyone would find they are on the same side.

2. Discuss differences with respect for the other person. This involves avoiding cheap shots like, "I can't believe you said that" or "You, of all people, should know better than that." Disagreement is no cause for attacking the other person like a political opponent. Even if we think the other person's idea is the most off-the-wall thing we've ever heard, it impairs relationships and cooperation to say so. Always, let the other person save face.

3. Remember that issues come and go, but damaging statements remain. Though we can apologize, and often should, we can never unsay something. Be careful in a discussion when the adrenaline is pumping.

4. Consider that we don't have to agree on everything to accomplish great things together. "Two heads are better than one" doesn't mean "two identical heads." It means even differing viewpoints can increase brainpower and creativity. When two heads always think just alike, one is expendable.

But, what do I know? It could be we differ with respect to how to handle disagreements. You may take another approach. Is it effective?

LEADERSHIP PRINCIPLE: When you disagree remain agreeable.

DEAL OR NO DEAL

"How much I owe you for the haircut?

"Well, let's see, what day of the week is it?"

This bit of foolishness often goes on between a customer and me, and usually produces the desired effect. A chuckle. This type of approach, though, has become an increasingly popular way of doing business and is not funny at all. It's irritating!

I once took Mom's car to have some minor service done. Her bill was $20. About a week later, I took my car in for what I thought was the same thing. But it cost me $30.

The difference? Well, I was not alert enough to say "no" to all the subtle add-ons.

Similarly, Sherry and I had lunch at a place that had an all-you-can-eat buffet and a discount plate. She was hungrier than I. So, she had the buffet. When we got to the table, and looked at the ticket, we discovered my discount plate cost about a dollar more than hers.

Why? I had tea. She had water.

Having gotten a bit out of character at the car place by telling them I didn't appreciate their let's-make-a-deal-flea-market way of doing business, I decided not to embarrass Sherry at lunch. And, I didn't want to appear cheap. I still didn't appreciate that way of doing business. Who wants to always have to keep their guard up and a pocket calculator handy every time they go in a business?

Such seems to be the new wave of businesses of all sizes. Have you gotten a cell phone lately? Or tried to figure out charges on a phone bill? It takes a cadre of Philadelphia lawyers.

Many years ago, my father, who liked to bargain, was in the market for old wagon wheels that he could use as trellises for his climbing roses. He pulled off the highway one day, where he spotted just what he'd been looking for. When the old timer walked up, Dad asked him his price.

"Wow, that's a little steep," Dad said.

"Then drive on," was the reply.

I have more respect for that kind of straightforward approach than for a lot of the wheeling-dealing (deceiving) that takes place. There's something to be said for the customer being able to easily understand the deal.

At J.B.'s, haircuts are $15 every day for everyone. Sometimes we get one who thinks that's too much. That's okay. At least he knows the deal. And, if we don't irritate him before he gets out the door, maybe someday we'll get the opportunity to fix the discounted haircut he got somewhere else.

LEADERSHIP PRINCIPLE: Treat people in the same honest, straightforward manner in which you wish to be treated.

THOSE ALL-IMPORTANT FIRST IMPRESSIONS

"You only have one chance to make a good first impression." How many times have we heard that? Regardless, it's very true! Studies have shown that new acquaintances form an opinion of us within seconds. And, if negative, it's very difficult to change that opinion. What can we do to improve our chances of making a positive first impression?

The first thing we can do is recognize that the objective is not to "impress." The objective is to "connect" in a positive way. There is a difference.

George Bernard Shaw was once cornered by a fellow who tried to impress him with his wisdom, and proceeded to talk incessantly. When Shaw was able to get a word in edgewise, he said that he was convinced the two of them knew just about everything.

"You," he said, "seem to know everything except the fact that you are boring me to death, and I certainly know that."

Ouch!

We've all likely been victims of someone who was trying very hard to impress us. Maybe we were even guilty of such. Whether it involves talking more, talking louder, being overly friendly or just being obnoxious it creates the opposite effect of what we really want. The key is to be relaxed and respectful.

To help us to relax and to make a good impression, it's wise to give attention to dress. Rocket science isn't required to know that there are different types of dress for various occasions.

However, common sense is required to know when to wear what. And, as a rule of thumb, it's generally better to overdress a bit for the occasion than it is to underdress. I recently attended a mixer at which I was the only man who wore a coat and tie. I would much rather it had been that way, though, than the reverse. It's much easier to connect when confident than it is when feeling inferior. Along this line, I might also add that, when it comes to spending money on clothes, it's better to pay more for quality and buy less. Quality shows and makes a better impression.

Eye contact also shows. In the blockbuster movie Karate Kid, there is a line that applies when interacting with others: "Eyes, eyes! Always look eyes." That has not always been easy for me, and may not be for you. Here is something that might help. Practice looking at your own eyes in the mirror. Then look at others by looking at the bridge of their nose. They will think you are making eye contact, and it's a start toward doing just that. Remember, if you don't look others in the eye they likely won't trust you. This is true in spite of the fact a con can look you in the eye while taking your last dollar.

It is also necessary to speak up when interacting with others. This doesn't mean yelling at people any more than eye contact means boring a hole through them. It simply means having enough volume to be heard and perceived as someone worth listening to.

As part of the baby boomer generation, I was taught "children are to be seen, not heard." As an adult, I had to train myself to be heard. Often I wore my watch on my right wrist instead of my left to remind myself to speak up. It makes a much better first impression. Conversely, it's not a good sign when the listener has to immediately ask you to repeat something.

Lastly, it's always a good idea to greet others with a smile and a warm handshake (if they wish to shake hands). Be genuinely happy to see the person, and show it. A pleasing voice, eye contact and fine clothes go for naught if the person inside really doesn't like people. If we do like people and are glad to see them we should tell our face because, more than anything else, others will read our face in forming a first impression.

LEADERSHIP PRINCIPLE: Be conscious of first impressions, but never seek merely to impress.

PRACTICAL STRESS ARRESTERS

I've often been asked if I get nervous before a speech. There was a time when I did. I like to think that now I get excited. There's a difference.

For a speaker excitement is a positive. Generally, a speaker who is cool as a cucumber is about as interesting. Excitement, though, puts fire into a presentation. Nervousness is negative and a distraction. If I got really nervous before every talk, it would become so stressful I'd either have to get over it or give up speaking. Such would be similar to stress in any endeavor. It would not only be distracting. It would be energy draining.

There are aspects of the speaking business that are sometimes stressful, just as certain things about your business might be. Life, itself, can be stressful. What are some steps we can take to relieve some of the pressure?

One of the stress relievers I've discovered is to focus on the task at hand. While there might be something to be said for multi-tasking, it can create stress. When the barbershop fills with customers, it helps to keep in mind that I can only cut one head of hair at a time. The same approach helps when it seems there are a million things to do to get ready to speak at a convention. Much like eating an elephant, it comes down to one bite at a time.

In close connection with single-tasking is to lower one's tolerance for stress. Have you ever noticed that those who say they have a high tolerance for stress are always highly stressed? If, on the other hand, we took the approach that we have a low tolerance for stress it might lead us to say "no" to additional commitments that only add stress to our lives. It might also cause us to delegate some of the responsibilities we've been carrying.

Additionally, in our efforts to reduce stress we need to sometimes lower our expectations. It has been said that opposites attract. If that's true, it gives a basis for why Sherry and I have stayed married 41 years. Her philosophy is, "Any job worth doing is worth doing state of the art." She would tell you that, with some exceptions, mine is not. This is not an attempt to criticize her. It's just to say in this respect we are different. My approach, however, greatly reduces stress in my life, and also frees me to get on with the things that really do need to be done state of the art.

Last, but not least, one of the steps we can take to reduce stress is to keep in mind that we can make a choice not to be stressed. Though others can certainly contribute to our stress, in reality it's a state of mind that we can control.

LEADERSHIP PRINCIPLE: Seek ways to decrease stress, while increasing quality of life and capacity for leadership.

HOW TO DEVELOP A SENSE OF HUMOR

Once, after a presentation in Las Vegas, I was asked how we develop a sense of humor. Because of what I'd said in the presentation, the lady seemed to realize that humor sells ideas, reduces stress and builds relationships—at home and in the workplace. Like most when they really don't have a very good answer, I responded, "That's a very good question."

Recently, I wished the inquirer could have been with me. Just by observation she might have gotten her answer.

It didn't start out as a red letter day. Sherry was feeling bad because she had not gone to bed at all the night before. She had been preparing for the first day of class following the holidays. My widowed mom had been having severe pain in her lower abdomen for several days. A dear friend since boyhood was in the hospital across town with pneumonia. Several months prior he'd had a stroke. And, with all this on the back burner in my mind, my brand new talk that I was giving that night was on the front burner.

Though I truly wanted to check on my sick friend, I wasn't looking forward to the drive across town and the maze at the medical center. Refusing to be deterred from what I wanted and needed to do, I left the office and got in the car.

Before getting on the highway, I pulled into Walgreen's to get some breath mints for me and shampoo for Sherry. As I neared the cash register, I realized how it might look for me to be standing there buying shampoo. So, in order to beat the cashier to the punch, I smiled and quipped, "I picked up this volumizing shampoo. I sure hope this stuff works because, as you can see, I really need it."

The poor lady lost it. She was laughing so hard I thought I was going to have to ring up my own sale. When she gained her composure, she called a friend over so she could tell her what the crazy bald guy had said. They were still laughing as I walked out the door smiling.

The first thing I did when I saw my friend in the hospital was tell him what had happened at Walgreen's. The first thing he did when his wife later walked into his room was have me retell the story to her. That night, after my talk, as I was chatting with friends I told it again. The next day, I repeated the story to customers. Now I'm telling you.

Admittedly, the next stop with my story is not "The Tonight Show." But, that's okay. Just knowing I brightened a day for myself and others is sufficient. What made it possible? Simply taking my focus off self and looking outward at life, standing on its ear.

When I said "That's a good question" to the lady in Vegas, maybe I really followed it with a better answer than I thought. What I told her was that we develop a sense of humor by looking outward, and that self-centered, anxious people are rarely funny.

By the way, though Mom was hospitalized, Sherry, my friend and my talk are no longer sources of concern. For the most part, as is often the case, I was anxious for nothing.

LEADERSHIP PRINCIPLE: Remember that the difference between turning our thoughts inward and turning them outward is often the all-important difference between self-pity and a sense of humor.

ACHIEVEMENT AT THE SPEED OF LIFE

The Norman Rockwell calendar, hanging on the wall beside my chair, told me that the day was March 24, 2005. It brought to mind events that had transpired exactly a month prior.

On February 24th, I was seated in the Cracker Barrel Restaurant, sipping my morning coffee. Though attempting to read a book, my mind kept alternating between thoughts of the speech I would give the next day and my mom who had been in the hospital for several weeks.

I planned to check on Mom at the hospital as soon as I finished my coffee. I would then catch a noon flight from San Antonio to New Orleans, where I would be taken by car across the causeway to Covington.

Suddenly, my cell phone rang. The doctor said Mom was not going to make it. It was just a matter of days. In 30 minutes, the phone rang again. It was the hospital. She had passed. Less than a month from the time she entered the hospital for a hysterectomy, cancer had taken her away.

I got up from the table, in stunned silence, and headed to the hospital. After tending to matters at the hospital, and after some calls to make preliminary arrangements, I boarded a plane for New Orleans. Two hundred and fifty people were expecting to hear someone called The Barber-osopher the next day.

After a night's rest, I felt I finally had it together. Breakfast was very relaxing. I went over my speech and did some reading. Afterward I borrowed a hotel computer and printed my boarding passes for the night flight back to San Antonio. Then I settled into a comfortable waiting chair in the lobby, while I waited for my ride to the meeting place. What happened next turned out to be the start of mishaps.

My cell phone rang. It was the lady in the sales office of the hotel. The same lady whose computer I had borrowed while printing the boarding passes.

"Mr. Sumerlin, you left your folder on my desk."

"The folder" was the one in which I had my airline information. It also contained my speech. Whew!!! I dodged the bullet there. I would have to have a much clearer head for the meeting.

The drive to the country club where the meeting took place was short, pleasant and uneventful. When the time came for the noon awards banquet, the place was packed. It was the largest crowd ever for the association. I was so excited I could thread a sewing machine while it was running. I didn't know at the time, however, that two hours later, when I got up to speak, half the crowd would have left to go back to work.

The meeting was scheduled from twelve to two. I was scheduled to speak from 1:15 p.m. to 2 p.m. However, by the time all the awards were presented it was 2:10 p.m. The meeting planner asked if I could cut my forty-five minute talk to thirty minutes. I assured her I could. Then the totally unexpected happened.

About two minutes into my presentation, while standing in front of the floor level podium, I noticed someone ease up to the podium. Apparently, the lady thought she needed to tidy up what had been left on the stand by previous speakers. She tidied up alright. To my horror, she took everything off the podium—including my four pages of notes! Suddenly I was left with half an audience, two-thirds of a forty-five minute speech and no notes.

Frankly, all that was really needed of the notes were the names of various attendees that I wanted to mention and the illustrative material that I was going to read for humor. Minus all of that, though, it was time for immediate adaptation.

If there ever was a time for the phrase "Never let 'um see you sweat," that was it. To panic would have meant disaster.

Please don't think that I think, because of all these obstacles, I did something special. I did what I was paid to do, and what any other speaker worth his or her salt would have done.

Furthermore, in your profession, there are probably days and circumstances that demand that you, also, suck it up. So, you call on experience, determination and professionalism — and just do it!

Many individuals received awards that day. Likely some achieved the things for which they were recognized in spite of various personal tragedies and repeated obstacles that no one ever knew about.

LEADERSHIP PRINCIPLE: Deliver – even under the most difficult circumstances.

THINK BEFORE YOU SPEAK

Someone has wisely said that words are vehicles on which thoughts travel. That being the case, we must always be careful what passenger we put on the bus.

For the most part, it seems we take the communication process for granted. We assume that since we have been talking since childhood we know how to communicate. Therefore, many give little thought to effective communication, or its by-products—good human relations and quality leadership. Maybe we could all use a few helpful reminders.

One of the things of which we must constantly remind ourselves is that effective communicating is always preceded by effective thinking. We're familiar with the adage about putting the brain in gear before engaging the mouth. It's good advice. Often the first words that come to mind are not the most appropriate ones.

Along the same line, thought often needs to be combined with delay if we are to communicate effectively. Long ago I learned that often what's written one day doesn't look nearly as good the day after. For that reason, I seldom submit a column the same day I write it. This practice has prevented untold embarrassment.

The same principle applies in other forms of communication. Who has not at some time thought they had the right response, only to think the next day, "I sure wish I hadn't said it like that?" Who hasn't fired off an angry e-mail, and then wished they hadn't? An immediate response is required much less often than we think. Next time, ask yourself, "What's the hurry?" Then give the words more thought.

For certain, by using the right words we practice better human relations. But, the right word choice is also an essential for clearer meaning. Consider the case of one who enters a fast food restaurant and asks them to cut the onions on her hamburger? Does she mean she wants the onions diced, sliced or eliminated?

If a man tells his barber he wants his hair cut over the ear, does he mean he wants the hair to cover a portion of the ear or does he want the entire ear to show? Sometimes what is crystal clear to the speaker is clear as mud to the hearer.

And, then, there's the element of voice inflection. What parent has not said to the child, "It's not what you said but how you said it that concerns me"? Voice inflection can convey meaning as surely as choice of words, and can even alter meaning. Because inflection and word choice are both so important to conveying an accurate message, sometimes practice is in order.

Though I'm not generally given to talking to myself (and when I do I never answer back), I often "talk out" a thought while driving. This is just to see how it sounds. And when this method is not satisfactory, I try the words out on an impartial listener. I then take note of the person's facial expressions and body language. Or, I just ask for a verbal response. Though the importance of the message would determine when such a practice is necessary, it's necessary more often than we think.

In all communication remember there are times when silence is an appropriate response. A proverb says that a fool speaks all his mind. Even though we might have an opinion, we're not always required (or even asked) to give it. And, if pressed for a comment, "no comment" often works very well. Knowing how and when to communicate are both signs of maturity.

LEADERSHIP PRINCIPLE: Beware of making good thinking a casualty of reckless words.

THE ART OF DEALING WITH CRITICISM

Have you ever been criticized? Webster says that to criticize is "to stress the faults of." It's synonymous with "reprehend, blame, censure, reprobate, condemn, denounce." Does that sound like anything you've ever experienced?

If you've ever done anything, you've been criticized. Likely the more you've tried to do, the more critics you've had. Since no one ever bothers kicking a dead dog, the only way to avoid criticism is to do nothing and to be nothing. Viewed from another perspective, rarely are residents of cemeteries ever criticized.

Realistically, we ought to be more surprised when no one finds fault than when someone does. If we're doing anything, criticism isn't a matter of "if," it's simply a matter of "when." Rather than internalizing it and being paralyzed by it, successful individuals learn how to effectively deal with it.

Foremost is the need to respond rather than react. If one reacts to something that is hot by withdrawing the hand, that's good. However, in interpersonal relationships reacting is generally not good.

Anger is a natural reaction to criticism. And, somewhat like taking a mouthful of hot coffee, whatever occurs after the anger is going to be wrong.

As an illustration of reacting to criticism, I recall something that happened following a presentation years ago. A gentleman walked up to me and, without even a fare-thee-well, said, "I disagree with you 100 percent." I felt that was an excessive amount of disagreement. I also found it very hard to like the fellow, and was even angered by his remark. If allowed to persist, this kind of anger would have led to resentment and, possibly, hatred. It would, then, have been extremely difficult to find anything at all in the criticism from which I might have benefited. Furthermore, experience has taught me that Harry Emerson Fosdick was right when he said that to hate someone is like burning your house down to get rid of the rats.

Actually, rather than reacting with anger or animosity, a proper response might be to consider that the criticism might have some merit. Looking back on the presentation, I could probably have done a better job making some points and could have left out others. Rarely is a particular criticism without any merit at all. It could be a basis for improvement.

In a manner of speaking, all criticism is a compliment. Either someone cares enough about us to say something that she thinks might be helpful, or someone feels we are in some way superior (a threat) and thinks she needs to attack. Either way, it's a good idea to look at the content of the remark, as well as the intent. Then, we are in a better position to respond appropriately.

Regarding a proper response, delay is often a good idea. Off-the-cuff remarks, made while hurting, are often like pouring gasoline on a fire. If an immediate response is necessary, "Thank you so much for caring and I'll give that some thought," might be as good as it gets.

As we attempt to deal with criticism in the home, on the job and in all relationships, maybe we should take from those experiences knowledge that might help us when we're tempted to criticize others. Knowing how painful such is for us to receive might cause us to refrain from eagerly finding fault in others. It might also help us to treat others like we want to be treated.

LEADERSHIP PRINCIPLE: Learn how to give and receive criticism and you'll likely go farther in life.

CONTROL THE CONTROLLABLE

It was mid-afternoon as I pointed my Sebring south out of Abilene on Highway 83, and headed toward San Antonio. Disappointment swept over me. Several months prior I had given one of the best speeches of my life. That was then. I was not pleased with what 250 people had just heard.

The previous day, the trip had started well. The decision to make the five-hour drive, as opposed to flying, had been a good one. The Hill Country was spectacular, the fried shrimp I had for lunch in Kerrville was delicious and Alan Jackson on CD was as good as usual. A time or two I stopped for coffee and reading. All of the things one cannot enjoy while shoulder to shoulder in an airplane, I had savored. It was a nice road trip.

The hotel accommodations were good. After settling in, I walked across the street to the mall, bought a book and sat down for a quiet read, while eating desert and sipping coffee. I kept a close eye on the time, however. I definitely didn't want to miss the Astros vs. Cardinals National League Championship Series game 2 on TV.

Back in the room, I had a nice visit with Sherry on the phone and the Astros won their game. I turned out the light and pillowed my head a happy man.

Sunrise brought an absolutely gorgeous day. It made for a nice stroll through the very quaint, restored downtown area, while I entertained thoughts of the afternoon speech. I was rested, relaxed and ready.

I arrived at the meeting place several hours early, thus allowing plenty of time to get a feel for the occasion. It was packed with a wonderful group of people. They presented awards, we had lunch and I was introduced. For some reason, things did not click. Though I presented the material to the best of my ability, my thoughts and trademark humor, to me, seemed labored.

As soon as I got in the car and headed home, analysis began. It didn't take long before I came up with a handful of reasons for feeling the speech did not go well. Those are just excuses, I thought. Thinking back to Astro baseball, I was reminded of a recent poor playoff outing by Andy Pettite. Pettite had a sore knee, so the media said. I'm confident he did not say his injury was the reason for his disappointing outing. He didn't get where he is by offering excuses. There's a lesson here, I thought. We must always improve if there's room for improvement, but never offer excuses.

As I continued thinking of two things I love, baseball and speaking, I recalled something I read years ago: If a major league batter gets a hit one out of every three times at bat, he's a huge success at the plate. Why should I expect to hit a homerun every time I speak—or do anything? What I should reasonably expect is what the group received—my very best effort.

In the midst of these random thoughts, another thought suddenly began to surface. I had based all of my conclusions regarding the presentation on perceived audience response. I didn't feel like I had connected. On a similar occasion when I had felt the same way, evaluations proved my conclusions completely wrong.

The absurdity of such "mind reading" suddenly took a humorous twist. I remembered two preacher friends, one who was preaching while the other spent the week in the audience. Through the series of sermons, the listener took copious notes every night. However, in the middle of the final sermon, he folded his paper, stuck his pen and paper in his pocket and just listened.

"What was wrong with that sermon?" his friend asked later. "Why did you take notes on everything I said, and suddenly stop taking notes tonight?"

"Nothing was wrong with what you said tonight," he replied. "It was great. It's just that my pen ran out of ink."

Bottom line is that I don't know for certain how my speech was received. Nor do I always know what a favorable reception looks like. As with many things in life, all I can control is the process—not the outcome. With respect to the process, I know I did my best!

LEADERSHIP PRINCIPLE: In most every undertaking, all we can do is put forth our best effort and then, without beating ourselves up, hope for a favorable outcome.

SOME TELLING THINGS ABOUT QUESTIONS

The teller at the bank had a question for me. I don't remember what it was, but I do recall she prefaced it with, "This may be a stupid question."

In an attempt at humor, I replied, "There are no stupid questions, only the search."

Don't worry if you don't get it. It didn't make sense to her either.

Maybe what I'm about to say will make more sense: Some questions don't show much forethought. While I wouldn't necessarily call them stupid questions, they do tend to reflect on the inquirer. And, from a leadership point of view, they certainly don't enhance a person's image.

One such question is the I-nodded-off-and-wasn't-listening kind. We've all heard this type. It's the sort of question that is often asked during a presentation. A hand will shoot up and, when recognized, the person confidently asks about something that was just covered or asserts something that the speaker just said. Similarly, in a social setting, someone might say that she grew up on Long Island, only to be asked, "By the way, where are you from?"

Since most of us have asked such questions, at some time or other, how can we avoid repeating the error? Beyond the obvious solution of better listening, we might try pausing to ask ourselves, "Am I about to ask a very dumb question?" Then, if we still feel a need to ask, but have doubts, we can preface our question with, "I'm so sorry. Did you already tell me...?"

Other questions that we need to avoid fall into the this-is-an-interrogation category. Here the problem is not always with what we ask, but how. These questions tend to be close-ended, and asked in rapid order, with little time for response or elaboration. Where do you work? What do you do? Where did you go to school? What does your spouse do? How did you meet? How many kids you have? Are they married? Have children?

The inquirer might have a sincere interest in the other person's responses. Yet, what is perceived is, "Why does he want to know?" When bombarded with such questions, I'm tempted to respond with, "Which question do you want me to answer?" or simply "Yes." Open-ended questions (that do not lock a person into certain responses), when nicely paced rather than rapid fire, are marks of a thoughtful conversationalist. The other kind can be rude and intrusive.

A third type of question we might want to avoid asking is the RCA-Victor-dog variety. Those who are old enough to remember playing phonographs and listening to records probably remember the RCA Victor record label. It showed a dog, with his head tilted toward the bell of the old time phonograph, inquisitively listening to the music.

That's kind of the way I am with some questions. What did he ask? These are the kind of questions that might be asked at a senate hearing. They have so many words, twists and turns that the hearer tends to get lost in the detours. And, as if that's not bad enough, there is usually a follow-up question that is just as bad or worse.

In this regard, it sometimes pays to rehearse or to write out a question just to be sure it is clear, concise and to the point. At the very least, maybe we should run questions through the "common-sense check" in our heads before we open our mouths. Remember, great questions can teach us great things. But they don't just happen. They require great thought.

One final observation: When asking questions, be sure to check reasons and motives. Is the purpose to learn about people, things or facts? Or, unfortunately, is it to get attention, to show how smart we are, to stump the speaker or just to fill the silence? In such cases, silence can be golden.

LEADERSHIP PRINCIPLE: Questions have a way of revealing class and intelligence, or a lack thereof.

SERVICE THAT'S BAD TO THE LAST DROP

I've been known, when asked the price of a regular haircut at J.B.'s Barber Shop, to respond by saying, "We sell exceptional haircuts for the everyday low price of only $15." There are other things you can get at J.B.'s, however, for free. For instance, we give away bubble gum, lollipops and ice cold sodas. Occasionally, I also give away my books and DVDs. And, let's not forget all the free advice. We guarantee it to be worth at least what it costs.

All of these free items are part of customer service and of going the extra mile. It seems like a proper business approach and we don't expect some sort of recognition for doing business in such a manner.

I've noticed, as I travel the country, that others apparently feel the same way. In many hotels and restaurants people go out of their way to be accommodating. In some places, I've been greeted by name from the time I register until the time I check out. At other times, I've received calls in my room from the front desk personnel who were just checking to be sure everything was okay. It's the kind of service that makes you want to keep doing business with them.

Conversely, there is a mindset that seems to fear the possibility of doing or giving anything extra in business. Unfortunately, we've all been recipients of such.

Some time ago, I was asked to speak in South Texas at a graveside service for a longtime friend. Because another close friend lived nearby, I made arrangements to meet him for breakfast before the memorial service.

Having arrived at the small town hotel prior to my friend's arrival, I approached the registration desk wearing a sincere tie and a smile.

"Hi, how are you?" I asked the lady at the desk. "I need to ask a favor. I'm meeting a friend here for a brief visit and wondered if we might have breakfast in the area provided for your guests. Since we are not guests here, we would be perfectly willing to pay you for two breakfasts."

"I don't think so," she replied. "If we did that, we might not have enough food for our guests." I wondered how hungry she thought we were. But, she was accommodative enough to call the franchisee regarding my request. She confirmed that we might eat way too much. The food was, indeed, for their guests.

Having learned many years ago that you can't reason out of someone what hasn't been reasoned into them, I decided to forget it and to go somewhere else for breakfast. However, since my friend had not yet arrived, I turned back to the lady at the desk with what I thought was a minor request: "Excuse me," I said, "my friend has not yet arrived. What if I buy a cup of coffee from you while I'm waiting?"

How do you think a reasonable person would respond to such a request? "Sure. There's no charge. Help yourself. Make yourself comfortable while you wait. So sorry about the breakfast thing."

Not that lady. However, she was consistent. She thought I might, also, drink up the coffee from the guests.

With this (and a similar incident with the same hotel chain) in mind, please answer the following multiple choice question: In future travels, given a choice between sleeping in my car and staying with this particular chain, do you think I will (a) sleep in my car, (b) sleep in my car, or (c) sleep in my car?

LEADERSHIP PRINCIPLE: Those who fear going the second mile will eventually be lacking opportunities to go the first one.

LEAD WITH HUMOR

It was a very busy Saturday morning. When I turned on the lights to open the shop, I saw five customers waiting for haircuts. My nose was running like a faucet, allergies had me sneezing my head off and help was not scheduled to arrive for another two hours. A general anesthetic would have been a welcomed relief!

The morning continued in much the same way it began— very busy and very stressful. Then came a break in the tension. It happened when a customer stuck his head in the door, looked around and said, "Terry, I think I'll come back in a little while." Something came to mind that made all the difference. On an impulse I jokingly responded, "Well, I'm leaving in 10 minutes." Every head in the shop suddenly came up, as if to ask, "What are you talking about?"

Quickly I said, "Just kidding. Nobody move." I laughed, they laughed and my tension was gone. Instantly, it became a rather pleasant morning of banter, as the time flew by—and the money rolled in.

Isn't it amazing what a little laughter can do? Not only can it relieve stress and make life so much easier and more enjoyable; it can positively impact business by helping us sell ourselves, our goods and our services. If you'll pardon another personal illustration, I'll reinforce what was just said.

I was recently invited to the office of a CEO. He thought I might assist him in putting together a speech he was to give to a non-profit organization. As I sat across the conference table from him and his assistant, the atmosphere was cordial, but rather formal. We talked about the content of his presentation and the proper use of humor. He seemed to like the fact that humor is a large part of my presentations, and that I would make it a vital part of his. We then talked about the fee for what he had in mind.

I couldn't tell exactly how he was affected by the figure. He'd have made a good poker player. But, I was determined not to flinch or to show insecurity regarding the amount. His response was simply, "Is this fee negotiable?"

Like a blind hog finding an acorn, my brain suddenly stumbled across something I thought he might like. I replied, "I'm not sure I understand what you're asking. Are you telling me you want to pay more than I'm asking?"

For a moment he just looked at me, as if to say, "What? You think I'm crazy?" Our eyes locked in silence. Then, with a laugh, he turned to his assistant and said, "There's that humor he was talking about. I like that!"

Bottom line is I missed the sale. Apparently, his board decided to do something else. However, someday this same CEO might need to hire a humorous motivational speaker. You reckon he might know someone to call when that time comes?

LEADERSHIP PRINCIPLE: Nothing sells us and our ideas better than a great sense of humor.

DON'T BE A HUMAN REACTOR

Most aspiring speakers begin by speaking pro bono to various groups. It provides necessary speaking experience, while building credibility.

I recall one such engagement many years ago. The presentation was for a ladies' group, meeting in the nearby town of New Braunfels.

Unfortunately, while cruising up Interstate Highway 35 that day, I had a blowout. It was not what I had in mind for the afternoon's activities. While drivers whizzed by, I stood by my car, considering the options: change the tire, possibly ruin a good suit and still be late for the meeting; or who knew what.

As I was pondering the situation, a young couple with a little baby pulled up in a pickup. "Anything we can do to help?" the husband asked. Though I had always thought you can't look sharp riding in the back of a pickup, I would gladly have ridden there just to get to the event. But, I didn't have to. I slid in beside the young lady and her baby, and was taken right to the front door of the meeting room. It was an incredible act of kindness.

As I walked in (late), the meeting planner immediately began to introduce me as the speaker. As subtly as possible, I told her what had happened and that I had to call my wife so that she could take care of my car before the police towed it. She hardly missed a beat with her intro, while I was scurrying around looking for a phone.

As I reentered the room, having completed my call, she said, "Here is Terry Sumerlin, and he will be speaking on 'A To Do List for Winners.' "

It was then that I heard something from some sweet soul that sounded very much like, "What could he possibly know about being a winner?"

Do you know what a conniption is? That's just about what I had right there! I nearly lost it. Then I realized that unless I thought of something quick, it was about to be the longest 30 minutes that I had ever spent before an audience.

"You," I told the ladies, "are sharing with me in a first time experience. In all the time I've been doing presentations of various kinds, this is the first time I've ever been late for a speech."

Then I told them what had happened, and that I had hitchhiked to get there. Before I said another word, they gave me a standing ovation.

Now why have I told this? Is it to say that I always say the right thing, that I always respond appropriately, that I never react harshly? I wish that were the case.

It is to say that on those occasions (which are all too often) when I'm inclined to react rather than respond, I'm reminded of this event in New Braunfels and of the value of responding.

Generally, responding is positive while reacting is negative. Exceptions to this might be in cases of immediate danger. But, even here there can be negative carry-overs. Mark Twain said that the cat that sits on a hot stove lid will never sit on a hot stove lid again. He added that it will never sit on a cold stove lid, either. Reacting often tends to distort the real lesson in an experience.

Where others are involved, reacting also tends to destroy credibility. D.A Benton, in her wonderful book *How to Think Like a CEO*, says that when you lose it, you lose—every time. Responding, on the other hand, gives one the satisfaction of knowing he/she chose not to handle the problem in an immature way. Conversely, some would do well to remember, "You're only young once, but you can be immature forever" (Larry Anderson, retired major league relief pitcher).

Reacting also tends to reduce management to the knee-jerk variety. A thoughtful response, on the other hand, involves thoughtful evaluations of people and suitable solutions toward the good of all.

LEADERSHIP PRINCIPLE: Those who respond rather than react generally have fewer regrets and more committed followers.

SERIOUS LESSONS FROM A LOT OF CUTTING UP

Have you ever heard something that you thought was pretty good advice that years later you discovered to be very good advice? I recently experienced such.

On July 25, 1956, my uncle J.B. opened his barbershop in Alamo Heights, a suburb of San Antonio. I began working there in 1989 and in 1993 purchased the shop from him. Last week we celebrated 50 years of continuous operation; with lots of cake and punch, commemorative pens, hearty gripping and grinning, numerous friends and customers and, even, coverage (twice) by the local newspaper. We had a grand celebration.

In the midst of preparation for the event, I began to think back over my experiences and what I learned in my 17 of the shop's 50 years. Even though because of speaking activities I spend less and less time in the shop, barbering has confirmed and reinforced many common-sense truths. They are principles learned through the years, from various mentors, and that I try to impart to others when I speak. Following are just a few:

- "The job does not give you the dignity. You take the dignity to the job." — Zig Ziglar

When I first bought the shop, I was proud of the fact that I owned my own successful business. Yet, when someone would ask what I did for a living, I would avoid telling them what kind of business I owned. Just that I owned a small business. Similarly, when those who heard me speak would ask if I had another occupation, I'd usually give them the same sort of dodge. I couldn't bring myself to tell them I was a barber. Professional speaking was far more dignified.

Then I began to realize the impossibility of being a happy hypocrite. It also dawned on me that, though there have been countless barbers in the history of the profession, there is only one me. Likewise, there have been countless professional speakers. However, like all professions, these professions are just what they are—professions. It takes people to give them dignity and uniqueness. Thus, Barber-osophy was born.

- "People never forget what you do for their kids."— Marshall Davis, old-time preacher

Many of those who attended our anniversary party had one thing in common: They got their first haircut at J.B's. Some of them are now grandfathers. In some cases this loyalty spans several generations.

Though many factors enter into this relationship, gentleness, kindness and patience with "first haircuts" definitely contribute to this lasting bond. Many times, young couples come in with a little fellow in arms. "J.B. gave me my first haircut," the dad will say. "We want to keep up the tradition."

- "Remember that a man's name is to him the sweetest and most important sound in any language."—Dale Carnegie

Almost before I got my tools set up that first day of work in '89, J.B. showed me his "name book." On yellowed pages in a clip board were names of customers and their identifying characteristics. As a former instructor of a course that stressed name memory, I learned and taught memory techniques. J.B.'s 50-year friendship with customers retaught me the importance of calling people by name. With names, customers often become lifelong friends.

- "People don't care how much you know until they know how much you care." – Zig Ziglar

If you were to ask some of our 40 or 50-year customers, "Honestly, have you ever gotten a bad haircut from J.B.?" — I'd be real surprised if no one said yes. This is not a reflection on J.B. It's just to say barbering is not an exact science, and people are not always at their best at anything. If, in fact, J.B. gave someone a bad haircut, why do you suppose the same fellow would keep coming back for so many years? Could it be because J.B. cares? Could it be because he calls his customers by name, asks about their kids and tells them, with dignity, "I enjoy barbering today as much as I ever did"?

LEADERSHIP PRINCIPLE: If you want lasting success, practice what's good for people.

TWO POWERFUL LITTLE WORDS

A customer told me of the day he and a friend were playing golf. When they returned to their cars, his friend had a problem: He had locked his keys inside his vehicle.

He called a locksmith, who arrived promptly. He quickly unlocked the door and announced, "That will be $100."

My customer's friend went into orbit. "I'm not paying you $100 to unlock my door."

The locksmith remained calm, as he very quietly pushed down the lock, closed the door and walked away. Before he'd gotten very far, he closed the sale.

Experienced salespeople can often relate similar, though not identical, experiences. The need is often so great and the person so desperate for the product or service little or no sales technique is required.

However, that's not generally the case. What too often is the case is that we lose sales because we forget very basic principles of persuasion.

I was reminded of these simple principles recently while reading Elmer Wheeler's classic, *Tested Sentences That Sell*. He, you may recall, is the fellow who is best known for the phrase "Don't Sell the Steak—Sell the Sizzle." The many principles he taught in persuading (not manipulating) a prospect, a child, a spouse or an acquaintance are timeless. Let's look at two of these basic techniques having to do with questions.

The first question is why. Though we never want to be like an interrogator, this word alone can often turn a self-centered bore into a brilliant conversationalist. For example, our spouse might say, "I had such an awful day at the office today." We might respond with, "Yeah, me too." Then we're set to take the floor with a litany of our own woes. If, on the other hand, we compassionately ask our spouse "why," we might help in ways we never anticipated.

Similarly, if a prospect says "I need to think about it," we might simply say, "okay." If we do, we'll probably miss the sale. "Why," on the other hand, could easily draw out an objection we can handle.

Focusing a customer on which option can also be an effective persuasive tool. Even if we get to the root of an objection with "why," persuasion can lose its effectiveness when the person is given a choice between something and nothing. It's like parents who ask a little boy if he wants a haircut, or a teenager if he wants to cut the grass. It makes "no" the easy and natural response.

Wheeler pointed out the need for always making the choice between something and something—never something and nothing. For instance, he taught the restaurant industry to ask customers if they wanted chocolate or vanilla ice cream on their pie. Not if they wanted it a la mode. His approach made a huge difference in profit on the sale of pie. It will also make a big difference in our powers of persuasion.

LEADERSHIP PRINCIPLE: When selling goods, services or ideas increase your effectiveness by increasing the use of "why" and "which."

CLOTHES CAN'T COVER THE NAKED TRUTH

One morning while having breakfast in a local restaurant, a close friend and real estate broker named Eddie related an interesting conversation he had while showing a home to a businessman and his wife. The conversation is significant because it reinforces basic leadership principles.

The gentleman who was looking at the home sells expensive suits to a very exclusive clientele. As you might expect, he was dressed accordingly. Eddie, on the other hand, chose some time ago to work comfortably (except for certain occasions requiring coat and tie) in Wranglers, a nice shirt, a Stetson and boots. He found their contrast in apparel rather interesting and humorously commented on it.

The businessman replied, "I would buy from you not because of the way you dress, but simply because I trust you." He added that in the South Texas heat, Eddie's attire is becoming somewhat the norm for businessmen.

For two reasons the conversation stimulated my thinking. First of all, I tend to subscribe to the old dress-for-success philosophy. I look like Howdy Doody in jeans and boots. The incident reminded me, however, that our dress should often be determined relative to where we are, who we're with and what we're doing. Secondly, as one whose presentations stress the importance of large trust accounts and impeccable integrity, I found the man's statement to be a practical confirmation of their importance.

As a reader, you possibly have strong opinions about what works for you in business attire. That's fine. Or you may have no opinion at all on the subject. However, this is about the far more important matter of trust and how it can be established.

One of the things I failed to tell you about the preceding conversation is something that led up to it. Eddie asked the prospect if he was a city councilman. Or, maybe a lawyer. The man said he was neither. "Why would you think that?" he asked. The answer had to do with his attire and his fluency of speech. The questions, though, had to do with making the other person feel important. It's an approach that's guaranteed to build trust.

John Dewey, one of America's foremost philosophers, said that the deepest urge in human nature is "the desire to be important." Though our other basic needs of food, water, sleep and sex are generally met, this one often goes unfulfilled. Therefore, if in what we do and say we sincerely make others feel important, we will in turn be making invaluable deposits in our trust account.

Integrity is also an invaluable deposit. It does a great deal of damage to our reputation and to our influence when we gain people's trust by making them feel important, only to betray it by failing to deliver. It, then, becomes apparent that we merely flattered them. The businessman knew my friend would do what he said he'd do, when he said he'd do it, how he said he'd do it. That's integrity. Not all of it, but certainly much of it.

Clothing decisions may be relative. However, somewhat like a good haircut, there is nothing relative about integrity. We either have it or we don't, and others can readily tell which is the case. If we don't have it, others will avoid us like they would a lousy barber.

LEADERSHIP PRINCIPLE: Gain and keep the trust of others by giving more attention to who you are than to what you wear.

POWER OF PERSUASION ISN'T IN STOMPING

"Have you written a Barber-osophy about that?" a friend asked. "If you haven't, maybe you should."

The customer was referring to a comment I'd made regarding a certain politician who was on television. It was during a Q & A at a state university.

I simply commented to my customer that as I listened I was appalled at how abrupt, flippant and somewhat rude the fellow was to many of the students. The Barber-osophy was suggested when I said it seems anyone who feels a need to be rude or abrupt to make a point is apparently insecure or unsure of his point.

It reminded me of the church janitor who found a draft of the preacher's sermon notes in the wastebasket. He noticed that in the margin beside one point was written, "Stomp loudly. Weak point."

Such an approach might fool some of the people some of the time, but it will ultimately weaken credibility. And, even when it seems to work, "A man convinced against his will is of the same opinion still."

In view of these observations, perhaps we should invest time in learning techniques that might favorably change another's will. Along this line, consider the lives of three of our nation's outstanding leaders and how they illustrate time-tested techniques of persuasion.

The first leader is Benjamin Franklin. Though he has a multitude of impressive achievements to his credit, one can't help being especially impressed with what Franklin achieved in self-discipline. For instance, when an old Quaker friend took him aside and told him that he was abrupt, abrasive and arrogant, he took definite steps to change.

In the *Autobiography of Benjamin Franklin*, he says, "I made it a rule to forbear all direct contradiction to the sentiments of others, and all positive assertions of my own. I even forbade myself the use of every word or expression in the language that imported a fix'd opinion, such as 'certainly,' 'undoubtedly,' etc., and I adopted, instead of them, 'I conceive,' 'I apprehend,' or 'I imagine' a thing to be so or so; or 'it appears so at the present.'"

He also said that when another proposed something he thought was in error, "I denied myself the pleasure of contradicting abruptly." He rather observed that in certain circumstances the person would be right, but in the present case there appeared to be some difference.

So, what's my point? Am I saying that in every situation requiring persuasion, and in every particular, we should adopt Benjamin Franklin's approach? Not necessarily. I'm simply saying that he is atop the list of our nation's greatest statesmen.

Perhaps the same non-abrasive methods of persuasion that made him one of the greatest diplomats in history would serve us equally well in our relationships. The other two American leaders I have in mind when it comes to powers of persuasion are Abraham Lincoln and Ronald Reagan.

Though they had many leadership traits in common, one such outstanding trait was the ability to persuade through relating a good story.

It's no secret that everyone loves a good story. What is lesser known is that studies show nothing has more power to win others to our way of thinking than a story. Unfortunately, we don't tell enough stories and, often, don't tell them very well. Reagan and Lincoln were masters of such.

They both told stories that were easy to understand and that had obvious points. Oftentimes their stories were humorous.

They were also succinct. In other words, they didn't ramble on for an hour and conclude by saying, "Well, to make a long story short." That, no doubt contributed to the fact their stories were memorable.

At this point you may be thinking, "Well, that's fine for them. They were gifted communicators. I'm not."

There may be some truth to that. Or, there may not. Regardless, you and I are gifted with something neither of them ever had—our unique experiences. With time and practice we can learn to diplomatically relate these, as well as other people's experiences, in our attempts to persuade others.

LEADERSHIP PRINCIPLE: Persuade without giving offense or arousing bitterness, by generously using diplomacy and effective storytelling.

A GUARANTEED "NO"

A customer once told me that by simply asking for an upgrade at check-in he usually flies first class. I thought that was worth remembering. After all, who couldn't do with two bags of peanuts and a whole can of pop? Seriously, first class means much more than outrageous rates for wider seats or for the privilege of getting on and off the plane first. Considering who is often in first class, it can be a great networking opportunity. Anyway, next time I flew I decided to give my customer's approach a try.

With the confidence that usually goes with ignorance, I asked the lady at the ticket counter, "Is there any chance I could get an upgrade?"

"I don't know," she replied." "What did you intend to give in exchange?" Apparently she expected air miles or something of that sort.

I flashed what I thought was my most winsome smile: "I guess just my charm and good looks."

If she thought I was kidding, she never let on. It's a wonder she didn't have security detain me. I later reasoned that because my customer retired as manager of the local office of the ATF (Bureau of Alcohol, Tobacco and Firearms) he likely receives preferential treatment.

This airport incident came to mind on Christmas Eve, as I stood at the registration desk in the nearby resort hotel. Because we had our family-time Thanksgiving, and our children and spouses had their own plans for Christmas, Sherry and I decided a resort-empty-nest holiday would be nice. An upgraded one would be even better.

As we pulled into a near-empty parking lot, our chances for an upgrade looked pretty good. So, at the desk I was peaking on confidence. Hoping that the lady behind the counter was peaking on generosity, I asked, "Is there a chance we could get an upgrade?" She saved Sherry the embarrassment of my "charm and good looks" line when she quickly said, "Let's see."

When we got to our room, Sherry opened the door. She was absolutely overwhelmed. Though in traveling I've seen a few hotel rooms I, too, was a bit overwhelmed. It was a gorgeous, luxury suite, with a maximum room rate of $1000. We got it for the basic online rate—and just for asking!

As we headed downstairs for lunch, we passed the desk and the young lady that had handled our registration. We made it a point to thank her profusely for the wonderful accommodations. Then I began thinking about what had happened, and continued thinking about it until Christmas evening when I sat down at the computer.

One of the first things that came to mind was if we ask for what we want, we run the risk of sometimes being told "no." That is unpleasant, yet rarely harmful or fatal. On the other hand, when we don't ask for what we want, the answer is always "no." So, what do we have to lose?

Such being the case, I began thinking of applications. For instance, how many sales do you suppose have been lost because the salesperson didn't just ask for the order? How about add-on sales?

How many times have we put up with a less than desirable table in a restaurant by not simply asking for a better one? How many serious "discussions" have occurred because we expected our spouses, children, staff or friends to be mind readers—when we should have candidly expressed what we wanted or expected?

We must always be courteous and reasonable in our requests, and grateful when they are met.

That said, remember this: A terrible thing happens when we fail to ask for what we want—nothing!

LEADERSHIP PRINCIPLE: To get what you reasonably want and expect, courteously ask.

BENEFITS OF CHILLING OUT

We were shocked when an ice storm virtually shut down our city for several days. Schools, offices, businesses, the airport and even barbershops closed. It was very strange. South Texas isn't used to such. And, judging from the comments I heard, no one wants to get used to it. Nor do most want to get used to doing nothing.

I once heard a speaker say he could not imagine anything worse than being forever confined to a rocking chair, with nothing to do. A few days of confinement confirms his statement, and certainly makes one appreciate having something to do, some place to go and a way to get there. Confinement accomplishes other things as well.

It reminds us that boredom is not fatal, and that we are not indispensable. How easy it is to think that if we stepped off the merry-go-round of life for a brief respite, society would crumble. After all, I'm the fellow who can stick his finger in water, take it out and leave a hole. Not so, though sometimes I might be prone to think so.

Another thing that not being unable to get out and about accomplishes is that it gives us time to get caught up and organized in the office—without guilt. I use the phrase "without guilt" because sometimes one should feel guilty about certain office activities, especially when they serve as very poor substitutes for more challenging and more needful tasks. Many salespeople should be making calls, in or out of the office, instead of rearranging things on the desk. Yet, they justify their procrastination by telling themselves they're busy. And, after all, they just can't work in an unorganized work area.

Confinement is also a great time for self-assessment. Somewhat like the fellow who tries to tell which way the train went by looking at the tracks, we often have very superficial means of looking at our own efforts. There is a constant need for us to find a quiet spot, open our calendar, planner or PDA and take an objective look at where we have been and where we are headed, what we have accomplished and how we plan to accomplish more. Down times such as during ice storms, brief illnesses, airport layovers and hotel stays are ideal for this task.

Lastly, when we can't go anywhere there's often opportunity for relaxation and reconnecting with our families. In view of the fact that studies have shown the average American parent only spends a few minutes per week one-on-one with his or her child, unexpected family time is not a bad thing. Since Sherry and I have an empty nest, the ice storm provided an ideal time for the two of us to simply chat and drink coffee in front of the fireplace, read, watch DVDs and just be carefree.

LEADERSHIP PRINCIPLE: To make the most of down time, avoid letting it get you down.

MY HIJACKER FRIEND

The flight was many years ago. So, I'm not sure about the origin or destination. I think it was Atlanta to Ft. Lauderdale, to board a ship out of Port Everglades. Though these details are unclear, the following story is not.

I was in the middle seat. I remember nothing about the person next to the window. The man in the aisle seat, however, I remember very well.

He appeared to be 30-something, was tall, trim, and had shoulder length, jet black curls. He was dressed casually (not power casual, just casual), and definitely not part of my crowd. He actually looked sort of international, and I thought could have been a hijacker looking for an opportunity.

During flight we exchanged courteous greetings and, with the exception of when I excused myself to go to the lavatory, nothing else was said.

The flight went very well, each of us doing our reading or napping, and in no time I was comfortably settled aboard the Princess ship. It's what happened at sea that was a bit unsettling. It taught me a valuable lesson.

One day as I was having breakfast in the 11th deck Horizon Court, who should I see but my acquaintance from the flight? I had seen him previously, but this time he walked over and struck up a conversation.

"What do you do on the ship?" he asked in a friendly manner. "I know you're not just a passenger because you seem to know your way around." I didn't tell him I learned a long time ago that first time passengers step off elevators looking around like they were just beamed down from Starship Enterprise.

I told him I was doing "enrichment lectures" for the passengers. He, in turn, said he was doing one of the nightly performances. Actually, he was an internationally renowned pianist. Not exactly the hijacker type, I guess.

As we became friends and visited several times over the next few days, I learned that he had a wife and two precious little daughters at home in Florida. I also found out that he spent six months a year performing in Europe and six months ship-hopping, doing one and two-night gigs. He had a very demanding, stressful schedule. But, he was very gracious and classy—a genuine delight to sort of hang with. When it was time for him to "jump ship," I was sorry to see him go.

To this day, though I no longer have his name or contact information, I think of how the time we were together was too short. I also think of how that time was made even shorter by my prejudice on the flight. We could have begun our friendship at that time. My prejudice and mistaken first impression were barriers. I'm not proud of that.

In this case, the price of prejudice (pre-judging) could ultimately have been a missed friendship. In other circumstances, it might be the loss of future business, a learning opportunity or a pleasurable experience.

How often do we assume because of someone's appearance, background, ethnicity, socioeconomic level or what have you, that any dealings with him/her would be harmful or a waste of time? How often, when someone disagrees with us, do we immediately start trying to figure out motive instead of trying to learn from the experience? How often does prejudice keep us from a pleasurable, though new, experience?

My friend's solo performance was just that—pure pleasure. As his black curls bounced gently on the shoulders of his finely tailored tuxedo, from center stage, he held us spellbound.

LEADERSHIP PRINCIPLE: Become a more effective leader by eliminating immature prejudices.

HOW TO EAT A FROG

As I sat in the examining room waiting for the orthopedic surgeon to come in, I kept wishing he would hurry up and just give me the verdict.

My sweaty palms served as a distraction from the seasonal allergies affecting my nose. I got a paper towel for my nose and considered washing the sweat off my hands before shaking hands with the doctor.

Then I thought if I would just read a book and relax my palms would dry. I'd hardly read one sentence when the doctor walked in.

As longtime acquaintances, we chatted for a few minutes before he began an examination of my left shoulder and the wear from years of barbering. Lest someone think my problem is just age, let me hasten to say my right shoulder is the same age as my left and it is just fine.

"The good news is," he said, "the MRI shows no tear, just an impingement. With an injection and some physical therapy you should be fine."

When I winced and groaned, he assured me that the cortisone injection was necessary to reduce inflammation, and that his assistant was a master of the procedure. It would be virtually painless.

Knowing how "virtually painless procedures" and "some discomfort" generally hurt like the dickens, I had my doubts. She was fabulous, however, and successfully brought to an end six months of anxiety.

Yes, six months! Can you believe that for six months I put off treatment and put up with pain? Not only that, but I also put up with an overactive imagination.

At one point, I actually thought I might have bone cancer, and then I downgraded the condition to one requiring rotator cuff surgery.

Yet, though the pain distracted me in nearly everything I did, I kept telling myself, "Oh, it's starting to feel better." I finally decided enough is enough.

Mark Twain said, "I am an old man and have known a great many troubles, but most of them never happened." Whether it involves our health, our business or our personal lives, problems left unsolved are fertile ground for the imagination. And, need I remind us, imagination is the strongest nation on earth?

How many times have we done similar things to what I did with my shoulder? How many times have we all let a problem distract us, while imagining all sorts of horrible outcomes? There is really no substitute for finding out all we can about a problem and then acting as soon as possible.

Mark Twain also said, "If you have to eat a frog, don't look at it for too long." How I wish I had taken his advice. For years I'd heard all sorts of negative things about cortisone injections. And, to quote W.C. Fields, "All things considered, I'd rather be in Philadelphia." Yet, it was really no big deal at all, and the assistant was wonderful. The procedure certainly didn't warrant all the anxiety, sweaty palms and procrastination in getting treatment.

Similarly, there are those who get all worked up over presentations, reports, job interviews, encounters and confrontations only to discover they wasted a lot of time and energy worrying about a frog they should have eaten immediately instead of trying to stare it down.

By the way, the book I took into the doctor's office to read as a diversion from my anxiety is called *Success Built to Last*, and I highly recommend it. When I picked it up off the table in the examining room and headed for the exit, I couldn't help thinking of the necessary link between success that lasts and common-sense problem solving.

LEADERSHIP PRINCIPLE: Don't stew on a problem long enough to give the imagination time to work, or time to distract from necessary problem solving.

TO GET A "10," BE A "10"

Before being seated for a delicious breakfast and fabulous sunrise on the lake, I decided to put my luggage in the car and check out of the hotel. I'd had a wonderful weekend as the keynoter for the Southwest Drycleaners Association in Clear Lake, Texas. The reception from attendees of the conference had been very warm, and the staff of the Hilton Houston NASA had been great.

When asked by the young man at the desk if everything had been okay, I assured him it had. "Then, Mr. Sumerlin, would you give us all 10s if we sent you an evaluation questionnaire?" I returned his pleasant smile and assured him I would. And, I did.

The questions were nothing out of the ordinary. You get the same basic survey from hotels all over the country. What you sometimes don't get is the kind of care I received there. And, I'm sure I was not the exception.

As a side note, the facility has an interesting history. It's the same hotel that made news some years ago when, right in front of the place, a dentist in a Mercedes put an end to her husband's affair by running over him.

The fact that she then put her car in reverse and backed over him might have had something to do with the jury convicting her. That said, what will always stand out in my mind about the hotel are those things over which the staff had and took control during my stay.

From check-in, I was tipped off regarding what to expect. First of all, I was greeted promptly and pleasantly. When asked if my room was ready for early check-in (since I wanted to rest prior to speaking in a few hours), the lady behind the counter responded, "Oh, yes sir. We received your call making that request and your room is ready for you."

After resting a while, I dressed for the event, and headed to the meeting room.

Hotel staff was setting up the room, but took time to pleasantly answer a few questions. They eagerly helped me with a few preparations, and asked how else they might help.

As we did a few odds and ends, I casually asked the audio/visual technician if he thought the weather was going to improve the next day. He said he didn't know, but would find out. Though I insisted it was not important, he left and came back with the weather report that he had printed off the computer. I was stunned by such a second-mile approach.

In addition to all this, there is the matter of the candy bowl on the registration desk. It was there when I checked in, but not there that night. The lady at the desk noticed I was seeking but not finding. "I told him," she said with a smile, "he shouldn't take that off the counter because someone would want it."

"We caught him," I replied jokingly. "But, I really don't need the candy."

She tracked him and the candy down, anyway, and returned the bowl to its rightful spot.

If you think these are all little things, you're right. If you think the focus of this column is just about hotel chains, think again.

"Can do," "How can I help?" and "going the extra mile" are all hallmarks of successful businesses. Often, they distinguish businesses or organizations that thrive from those that die.

One other quality of successful businesses is a well-trained staff that cares enough to seize an opportunity when one is presented.

"Cares" is the operative word. That's quality. And, while training might be helpful in many areas, training for overall quality of attitude is generally short lived and ineffective.

LEADERSHIP PRINCIPLE: Hiring quality people with a good attitude is by far superior to expecting all quality to come from training.

SPLAT! THE ULTIMATE SUCCESS TEST

Longtime customers at J.B.'s Barber Shop know if they want to get me fired up, all they have to do is ask about one of two things: my speaking schedule or the Houston Astros. I live and breathe public speaking, and suffer along with the Astros.

Sherry and I became Astro fans about 30 years ago, when we lived in the Houston area. Games became family outings. On one such an occasion, Houston was trailing by one run in the bottom of the ninth.

Our daughter Jo Ellen, who was a grade-schooler at the time, jumped up and hollered, "Jose Cruz, hit a home run!"

She was so pleased with herself when on the next pitch he hit a two-run home run to win the game. We've been huge fans ever since.

This particular season we've followed their early struggles and wondered what they might do to improve their offense. Management decided they needed to bring up Triple-A wonder Hunter Pence as a replacement for center fielder Chris Burke, who was struggling at the plate. Because of Burke's popularity with fans and teammates, sending him back to Triple-A was a very unpopular move.

This is the same Chris Burke who was on top with Astro fans when he hit a solo home run in the bottom of the 18th inning to end the longest post-season game in Major League history and clinch the National League Division Series over Atlanta on Oct. 9, 2005. Since then, he's had the inside track—until his bat let him down.

Those in the know seem to think that in time Burke will be back to the majors, if not with the Astros, with another team. Right now the young man is understandably crushed.

"I'm very upset," he told the media. "This is very hard, very difficult for me to accept. There are so many things going through my mind right now."

I feel for him. He seems like a fine person and such a hard worker. I can't help wondering, though, if one of the things going through his mind should be: "That's life."

That is also the path to success.

Hunter Pence, the young man that is now playing center field, sometime, somewhere, somehow will discover the same truth. Success is not without bumps, bruises, disappointment, discouragement and heartache.

Nonetheless, whether we lose our job, get demoted, don't get the job we wanted, experience financial disaster, have health problems, are disappointed by others or stabbed in the back—we can still succeed. We may simply be on a long, difficult road to a caliber of success that will one day truly be worth the pain.

One of my favorite stories involves a young man who was walking along a path, when he encountered a bearded old sage. He asked the wizened old gentleman, "Which way to success?" The old man just pointed down the path. The young man headed off in that direction.

Suddenly, there was a loud splat. The seeker returned to the sage all bruised and battered, yet with the same question. "Which way to success?"

Once again he just pointed, and again there was a loud splat. Yet, this time it was worse than before. The young man returned battered, bloody and barely walking. But he persisted. "Which way to success?" he asked the third time.

Before the response, the young man said, "Don't point. Talk."

"Success," the old man said, "is just past splat!"

Many are they who would have success without splat. They possibly look at what you do as glamorous, or you may look at what they do that way. "I wish I could do what he/she does" we sometimes whine. However, are we willing to do what she did in order to do what she does?

I once told Sherry that I knew I would make it as a professional speaker because I'd already tried and discarded everything that won't work, including near bankruptcy. Yet, though at long last I have reached a certain level of achievement, I dare not, you dare not, and Chris Burke dare not think we have experienced our last splat on the path to success.

LEADERSHIP PRINCIPLE: Success can be oh so sweet, but only if we refuse to allow the splat to make us oh so bitter.

THOSE WHO GET STEAMED TEND TO GET BURNED

I enjoy people watching. In fact, I'm more observant of people than of places and things.

Airports, I've found, are great people watching places. Especially is this true of airport coffee spots with seats that face traffic areas. Restaurants are also great places for observing people, and thus make for an interesting aspect of travel.

One morning while having coffee and a bite to eat at a fast food place we frequent near our home, people watching produced some interesting human relations observations.

All was quiet when suddenly a young professional in heels and a business suit stormed in. "Do you have someone working drive-thru?" she blurted out to all at the counter. "I've been sitting out there 10 minutes. I go through this every morning and I'm tired if it."

We didn't really hear what she was told by the manager. Apparently it wasn't what she wanted to hear because after angrily walking past our table and out the door, she came right back in. I wondered if we should duck, and from the expressions of the other customers, they were probably thinking the same thing.

"I want the phone number of the owner," she demanded.

As she stormed out **again,** I commented to Sherry, "I guess she got her day off to a lovely start."

Likely she had ruined her entire day by significantly raising her stress level. The spectacle she had just made of herself would probably replay in her mind throughout the day. And, of course, she would feel a need to relate the scene to all who would listen. All the while, her stinking thinking would increase with each telling of what an awful thing happened first thing that morning.

Since, as she said, she put up with that every day you wonder why she didn't just avoid the problem and go somewhere else. Was she on a mission to whip this establishment into shape? While it might be nice that she had such a high calling in life, it seems highly unlikely she would ever get five star service from a one star business. But, of course, she wasn't paying five star prices either.

Perhaps what she really wanted was a feeling of importance from telling someone off. If she got that, it was about all she accomplished. The employees blew the incident off with hardly a second thought.

All of such raises a question: From a human relations point of view, what might the lady have done that would have been wiser? No doubt, she had a legitimate complaint. What might have been a better course of action?

In all confrontations, calmness helps, as well as lowering the voice. Talking to the right person privately, rather than creating a public scene, also helps.

Perhaps in situations like this one, though, the best approach of all is to weigh what we stand to gain through the confrontation versus what we stand to lose through stress. We must recognize going in that some situations are no win and are best just tolerated or avoided, because when it comes to self-control:

LEADERSHIP PRINCIPLE: When we lose it, WE lose—every time.

A FUNNY THING HAPPENED WHILE IN LOVE

Our youngest daughter, Amanda, and I had just finished a wonderful lunch of Mexican food. She then dropped me off at Dallas Love Field for my return flight to San Antonio, and she returned to work at the Morton H. Meyerson Symphony Center. I had several hours on my hands before departure.

As usual, I decided to check out the bookstore. While scanning the titles in one corner, I overheard a lady who was seeking information from a gentleman in the opposite corner.

"Is this a bookstore?" she asked.

He assured her it was.

In the process, he cleared up something for me: What if it's not a bookstore and I've wandered into Victoria's Secret by mistake?

After she left and was out of earshot, I asked the fellow if she had indeed asked him what I thought she had. He confirmed that she had. He added that he might have taken offense to her question since he is vice president of the company, in charge of book sales.

"Something must be wrong with our manner of presentation," he said, "if she can't tell we're selling books here."

We then shared a laugh and chatted a moment as he responded to some questions regarding book sales in airports.

Back to the lady and in her defense, not everyone observes the same things or draws the same conclusions from what they (don't) notice. Also, we've all asked our share of ridiculous questions. I don't even have to be travel weary to do so. That said, the incident is still an amusing glimpse of human nature. People really are funny!

Something that had me primed to find this especially amusing was that it perfectly illustrated what I had just told a group a few hours earlier. While speaking in Fort Worth that morning at a joint regional conference for Senior Field Representatives of the U.S. Census Bureau, I had stressed the importance of a sense of humor in team building and leadership. I pointed out that humor is all around us—that life and people are funny. And, that a sense of humor tends to add to our credibility as leaders.

Yet, the only way we notice such humor (and by noticing develop a keen sense of humor) is by changing a self-absorbed, self-important attitude into an open, caring one. In other words, it helps to lighten up instead of taking ourselves so seriously.

In the process of finding life's lighter side, as leaders we should constantly seek opportunity to share this side of life with our team members. As illustrated with the VP in the bookstore, the human relations benefits can be powerful.

When I first noticed the gentleman, he was kneeling on the floor, heavily perspiring in a small area while checking his book inventory. He didn't appear to be having great time. After we shared a laugh and chatted a bit, a new type of atmosphere was created for both of us. When I left, he had a smile on his face, while bidding me a very pleasant day. I, too, wore a smile as I went on my way, feeling a bit less travel weary.

LEADERSHIP PRINCIPLE: To improve the quality of your own life, use humor to improve the lives of others.

WHEN THE HEADLESS HORSEMAN
DRIVES A TOWN CAR

We sometimes hear people say they're afraid of flying. Actually, I'm more afraid of taxicab rides. It's not the ride, itself, that scares me. I'm always concerned with the drivers knowing where they're going.

Recently, after speaking in Fort Worth, Texas, I needed to go to the Morton H. Meyerson Symphony Center in Dallas. So, I asked the bellhop to call a cab.

"Would you prefer a nice Town Car?" he asked.

I said "sure," and he proceeded to call someone he recommended.

Shortly, a beautiful new Town Car pulled up in front of the hotel. Impressive! As I got in I was even more impressed. It still had the new smell. Really nice! I got an uneasy feeling, however, when the driver got behind the wheel with his MapQuest page from the bellhop still in hand. Like the headless horseman, he took off in every direction.

I learned long ago there are certain people that you really don't want to say "oops." On a list of such folks, surgeons and barbers would have to be near the top—along with cab drivers.

When the gentleman got off the freeway and did a turnaround I figured he might be a bit confused. A short while later when he took the wrong exit ramp, and "oops-ed," I knew we had a problem. It was at that point he confessed he couldn't get me there.

"What do you want me to do?" he asked.

Not knowing what else to say, I suggested he take me back to the hotel and let me start over with another driver. Then I thought, surely he's not so lost he can't get us back.

Thankfully, he wasn't. And, the second ride was much more successful.

Every time I tell this story to friends—after they get through laughing at the oddity of the situation (after all, how often does a cab driver just give up?)—they want to know if the guy charged me for the ride.

Actually, he said nothing about a fare. However, I tipped him $10. Does that surprise you? It shouldn't. It merely proves something I learned from Zig Ziglar: "People don't care how much you know until they know how much you care."

The poor cab driver had only been on the job a week. Apparently, he had just been making runs from the hotel to the airport. He was obviously confused but, also, very embarrassed and very apologetic. I felt very badly for him. He tried his best, he failed and then he admitted his mistake. What more could he do?

Well, I guess he could get more training. But, he seemed to know he needed that without having to be told. I'm more concerned, on the other hand, with those we see every day who need more training and don't know it and don't care. Or, with the companies who train as little as possible because they figure their employees will eventually leave anyway and will take their training elsewhere. It makes you wonder how their customers feel about the company's employees who are untrained but stay.

Beyond what we've just noticed from this incident regarding those who care and those who don't, the situation also points out another significant lesson: Though a product or service may look and smell so new, sometimes the well-worn old standard serves us best with the least amount of aggravation.

The man driving the yellow minivan said he'd been driving for 20 years. "You can't name a place in Dallas or Fort Worth I can't find," he said proudly. Shortly, he found the front door of the symphony center and never once hesitated.

By the way, as did the first driver the second one also cared. But, he also knew what he was doing. That's a combination that's mighty hard to beat—anytime, anywhere.

LEADERSHIP PRINCIPLE: Success generally comes to those who care—and know what they're doing.

LEADERS KEEP LEARNING

Following is an excerpt from a talk I gave in Little Rock, Ark., on Oct. 25, 2007:

I have a soft spot in my heart for educators. This is primarily because I'm married to one. Sherry teaches 10th grade math.

But, I also feel this way because I know what a tremendous difference education has made in my life, and the difference it made in the lives of my parents.

Eddie Sumerlin, born April 6, 1922, was one of 12 children. He had only four or five years of formal education, because his parents needed him in the field instead of in the classroom.

He left the farm when he joined the Navy, and became part of "The Greatest Generation." He served courageously aboard the aircraft carrier USS Saratoga and was awarded the Purple Heart.

I didn't know he received the honor until I began gathering information for my remarks at his funeral about five years ago. What I knew was that Dad had come home from war; married Darlene Sanders, his 16-year-old sweetheart, one month shy of her graduation; gone to work; reared two sons—and tried to forget.

Decades later, as Dad neared civil service retirement, he saw an opportunity to better his and Mom's circumstances. Having been an automobile mechanic at Brooks Air Force Base, San Antonio, Texas, he had a chance to retire as supervisor of vehicle maintenance for the entire base. All he needed for the promotion was a high school diploma, which he (and Mom) didn't have.

They decided to attend adult education classes. It was a proud moment when, together, they received their GEDs.

It increased their self-esteem and greatly improved their immediate and future circumstances.

Looking back to the time when I was in school, I recall a good home where Mom and Dad took an interest in our education. However, I don't recall education being a huge priority. I do recall that through substantial financial sacrifice, Mom and Dad put my brother and me through barber school (thus giving us a trade) and felt we could pay our own way through college.

When I enrolled in San Antonio College, I was in for a rude awakening. I was told I would have to enroll in a non-credit remedial reading course in order for my registration to be accepted. I came out of high school reading 180 words per minute with 50 percent comprehension. I was virtually illiterate. Though I now read several books per month, I completed only one or two books my entire 12 years of school.

I argued that I wanted to take only credit courses, though I had no idea how I would get credit for classes I couldn't pass. But, having no choice in the matter, I took the reading course.

It was so eye opening that I then took the more advanced course, and have been reading "everything" I can get my hands on ever since. It truly changed my life.

Though I graduated Magna Cum Barely from San Antonio College, I did graduate. And, though in high school I graduated in the half of the class that made the top half possible, that has all changed because of good educators.

What I do now as a writer and speaker is because, from educators like you, I learned how to learn. It's also because I have never stopped learning. Be proud of what you do for our society as a professional educator.

... Thus went my recent presentation (not verbatim) to the 350 conference attendees of the Arkansas Association for Adult and Continuing Education, and I meant every word of it. What I didn't say, but should have added, is two-fold.

First of all, Henry David Thoreau said, "Formal education will make you a living. Self-education will make you a fortune." Likely what he had in mind is that learning is to never stop. It is a do-it-yourself project that has created great fortunes for many.

The second thing is that we are not rewarded for what we know, but for what we do with what we know—as it relates to others. They, in turn, determine how much our knowledge is worth!

LEADERSHIP PRINCIPLE: Be invaluable to others by always learning and by wisely using what you learn.

TEAMING UP WITH CHARACTER AND COURAGE

Legendary manager for the New York Yankees Charles Dillon ("Casey") Stengel said the key to his managerial success was his ability to keep the players that hated him away from those who were still undecided. Though Hall of Fame type players certainly didn't hurt his chances for success, it's hard to argue with his strategy.

If, on the other hand, you are part of a team with less than satisfactory management, what can you do? Though you might take a position elsewhere, it's not my place to make that kind of recommendation. What I would recommend is that, despite the circumstances or the managerial style of the decision makers, we must always stay true to our values.

There are circumstances where we must individually and courageously take a stand—especially in cases where we are asked to sacrifice character or conscience for the team. Cal Ripken Jr., faced this type of challenge.

It was 1994 and Major League Baseball was on strike. Yet, Ripken showed up at the ballpark every day, just as he'd always done. When asked what he was doing, he replied that he had signed a contract to work. He was there to honor that contract.

I have an idea that in addition to not sacrificing character for team play, neither would he have sacrificed dignity. He would not have tolerated certain treatment. Along this line, we must take a stand when our dignity is at risk because of that which is demeaning, disrespectful or unfair. In such cases, we must stand up and tell "the team" or management, "I will not accept that kind of treatment."

On the other hand, we must always understand that the job does not give us dignity. We take the dignity to the job.

Furthermore, as Eleanor Roosevelt said, "No one can make you feel inferior without your consent." In other words, sometimes we place too much value on what others do or say with respect to our dignity, and accept too little responsibility for determining our own thoughts.

Another area we might consider when we think of taking a stand for self rather than going along with the team might be that in which the price demanded by the team is unreasonable or more than one can afford to pay.

For instance, 12-to-15-hour workdays might occasionally be all right while on special projects. If such is required nearly every day, that might be too high a price to pay for success. It could be time to take a stand. Though many on their death bed might want more time with the spouse or children, rarely do they wish for another hour in the office, on the computer or on the cell phone. When quality of life is sacrificed for the team, or worse yet, for material possessions, it's time to say, "I'm not going to do that."

LEADERSHIP PRINCIPLE: Truly successful people have the courage and character to stand alone when they must.

THE BIGNESS OF SMALL TALK

At a dinner program on dining etiquette, the presenter pointed out that career-wise such matters are becoming more and more important. With increasing frequency, job interviews are taking place over formal lunches and dinners. Many corporations want to know before hiring someone how she might represent them in business settings.

In addition to what our speaker said regarding dining manners, I was intrigued by another comment: That small talk is a valuable part of the fine dining experience. That said, she then gave us time to chat with our table partners.

As I turned to the very nice lady seated next to me, she commented that small talk is not one of her favorite things. I commented that I felt the same way until I read that we generally don't get to big talk without going through small talk. It changed my point of view.

For many years, small talk has been a large part of my day. No place is there more of it than in a barbershop.

Yet, some of what takes place in a barbershop and elsewhere is more in the realm of useless talk than it is small talk. "What's the difference?" you might ask. The difference it seems is that, while all useless conversation is small talk, not all small talk is useless. Also, useless talk sometimes serves as polite conversation.

On the other hand, at its best, small talk has a purpose, a sense of direction and is planned. To say the least, forethought is involved. With it we're getting acquainted, seeking information, establishing a common bond and positioning ourselves for bigger talk.

In view of such, with effective small talk, we ask meaningful questions—questions that produce answers that we care about. To ask questions to get answers we don't care about is insincere and a waste of time.

For instance, I might casually comment that it's a beautiful day or that we're getting some badly needed rain. However, I don't normally talk about the weather or ask questions about it. First of all, we can't do anything to change the weather. Secondly, I don't have a burning interest in any answers I might get to questions about the weather. So, why ask?

With effective small talk, though, we not only care about the answers, we also ask good questions.

We don't ask the same questions every time we see the same person. Nor do we come across as conducting an interrogation. We're simply engaging the other person in conversation, with a view to connecting and getting to know him or her better.

Following are questions, in the form of open-ended statements, that seem to work well in this regard:

Tell me about your family. Most have a family, right? Yet, we don't want to ask if a person is married. That might make for an awkward response. "Family" gives the respondent lots of options.

Tell me about where you went to school. Because some did not go to college, "school" is a better term.

Tell me how you spend your time. In today's society, "Where do you work?" might create the embarrassing answer of "I'm unemployed." Or, it might say that we're unaware there are those who are independently wealthy and don't have to work.

Tell me about your recent travels. This often produces stimulating conversation.

With all of these "questions," and more—listen. Ask follow up questions, such as when, where, how and why. Also, a connection can often be made with, "Do you know Mr. ...?"

The main thing to remember with small talk is to think, in advance if possible. Plan to be engaging. The benefits can be delightful and far-reaching.

LEADERSHIP PRINCIPLE: To get to the big talk, learn the skill of effective small talk.

THIRSTY HORSE SUCCESS

Nearly every morning I'm in the barbershop, I walk across the street to the convenience store to get a snack or two. One morning, as I was waiting in line at the register, the cashier scanned the purchases for the customer in front of me. When she came to his coffee, she entered the amount manually. Seeing the amount on the screen, he immediately reacted rather strongly.

"Naw! Take that off," he said. "I'm not about to pay ninety-nine cents for a cup of coffee." The cashier, without so much as a change in expression, took off the ninety-nine cents.

However, it's what happened next that is a commentary on human nature.

The customer asked for a few lottery tickets. Evidently, they weren't overpriced.

As the gentleman headed out the door, I stepped to the counter and smiled at the familiar face behind the register.

"Don't say a word," she said.

"You know what I'm thinking," I replied.

"Yeah, I know what you're thinking," she said with a smile. "Don't say it."

We laughed, and I left—without saying a word. But now I will.

First, a word about perceived value. When, as a boy, I would agonize over whether I ought to spend a certain amount of money on a certain item Dad would say, "Son, it's worth whatever you're willing to pay for it."

Similarly, the difference in the value of a cup of coffee and of a lottery ticket (as well as many other things in life) is the difference in who's buying. Though it's none of my business whether someone buys a lottery ticket or not, personally, I wouldn't give two cents for one. On the other hand, I've been known to pay several bucks for coffee. People have different values.

Second, people are motivated by different things. I once read of a salesman who made no sales for the day. When questioned by his sales manager, his response was, "You know what they say. You can lead a horse to water but you can't make him drink."

His manager wisely responded: "You have it all wrong. Your job isn't to make the horse drink. Your job is to make him thirsty."

The convenience store customer was thirsty for the lottery tickets because he saw the possibility of gain. To him, there was a strong WIIFM (what's in it for me). If the man could have been persuaded that buying the coffee would have satisfied a need stronger than mere physical appetite, I'm confident he would have been "thirsty" and the price would not have been too much. In my case, making me "thirsty" for a lottery ticket would be an impossible job.

Lastly, the incident brings to mind how people have different likes. I've often thought that if everyone had the same likes, every man would want to be married to my wife.

From another perspective, maybe nobody would want to marry her.

For such reasons, the convenience store brews many different flavors of coffee to suit different tastes. They also have different products to suit different priorities.

LEADERSHIP PRINCIPLE: Those who would sell their goods, services or ideas must first understand the values, motivations, needs and likes of others.

HOW TO SHORT-CIRCUIT BUSINESS CONNECTIONS

St. Louis in February is quite different from San Antonio in February. I recently discovered that while speaking in the city of the Arch. I'm not at all used to thirteen degrees and eight inches of snow. However, from the Starbucks inside the hotel it was nice to look at the street corner and the winter wonderland.

What was even nicer was that I hit the "winter window" just right for driving. Yes, driving! Normally, for the sake of time and convenience, I fly to engagements. (Did I just use "convenience" and "fly" in the same sentence?) But, on this trip I wanted to stop in Dallas and Oklahoma City to see the kids and grandkids. I also wanted to see a dear cousin in Springfield, Mo.

The "winter window" I mentioned refers to the fact that, though the weather was rough during my stay in St. Louis, going and coming the weather and roads were fine. So, I was able to successfully combine pleasures of family and business.

The cousin part of the family, and my visit with her, is actually the reason for telling this story. What happened occurred while I was seated beside her in church.

Just before Sunday school, my cousin introduced me to a sweet lady seated beside her. We chatted a bit, and then class started. After class we chatted some more. I asked a few questions and discovered the lady is a distributor for some sort of formula you drink that does all kinds of good things for you. When she asked what I did I briefly told her, "I'm a speaker on my way to a conference in St. Louis." What happened next, I'll long remember.

"Do you have a business card?" the lady asked.

"Sure," I replied, confident that she was going to pass my contact information along to a meeting planner with her organization. I just knew I would be speaking to thousands of distributors in some exotic place.

To my surprise, she simply flipped the card over, wrote her contact information on the back and handed it back to me. "Give me a call," she said, "if you ever need any product."

After that I could hardly concentrate on the sermon. I also couldn't wait to tell someone what happened. I'd collected my latest Barber-osophy story.

When I got to the conference for Unigroup, Inc., I took the story out of the box for the first time, and related it during a presentation on connecting. I then asked the group, "What did she do wrong?"

"Everything," someone replied. Then we spent a few minutes discussing some specifics.

First of all, there is a time and a place for everything. Church is hardly the time or the place for what she did. Especially to a visitor!

From a personal point of view, on those occasions when friends where Sherry and I are members ask to buy my books and when I deliver them at church, I always make it a point not to receive payment there. I just believe good businesspeople (connectors) know when and where to do business.

Secondly, though now it's funny, she actually insulted me in the improper handling of my card. Good connectors receive a business card in such a manner as to show respect for the person giving it. The person's name is on the card. You should take a moment to look at the name. Then, carefully put the card away as if you've just received a treasure. We should never allow the other person to feel as if we think the card is just a piece of scratch paper.

The third thing we noticed in the session, regarding the story, is the most obvious: carry your own business cards. Though, as we said, there is a time and a place to use them — never be without them.

When it comes time to hand someone a card, be sure the print is toward the person so that she can immediately read it. Then place it in the person's hand as if bestowing a gift.

LEADERSHIP PRINCIPLE: Connecting minus respect and common sense equals cheap manipulation.

THE LUCKY DAY APPROACH

Though San Antonio temperatures have turned summer-like, the mornings have been absolutely incredible. In fact, I recently commented to a customer that perhaps I should hit the golf course.

I was reminded of a friend who got hit on the golf course. His experience reinforces something we all know but tend to forget: Attitude makes all the difference in how we appreciate the positive and respond to the negative events of life. That, in turn, often determines our success or failure.

The incident to which I referred in conversation with my customer, and that illustrates our principle, happened several years ago while playing on the beautiful Del Lago Golf Course in the Houston area. It was a nice fall South Texas morning. Well, as nice as 95 degrees gets in mid-September. I'd already spoken four times in two days, and was to speak two more times before heading home. A round of golf with good friends sounded like a great way to relax. The way I play golf, I probably should have chosen to relax over a good book.

We had played several holes and were having a great time, when we came to a 150-yard par three. All three of us hit our tee shots and were getting ready for our second shots. Since we were playing more slowly than the two fellows behind us, we decided to let them play through.

We were watching for the ball. Don was standing off to the left of the green, Robert was standing on the green and I was to the right, sitting in the golf cart. We saw the fellow hit. But, we never saw the ball.

Whack! Suddenly, I heard something that sounded like a hammer hitting a two-by-four. Then I saw Robert grab his head. I was terrified, and fully expected my friend to go down. He never did. As I covered the short distance from the cart to Robert, not knowing in what part of the head he'd been hit, the unthinkable flashed through my mind.

The ball had hit him, on the fly, just above the temple. Fortunately, he only received a small gash and a large bump on his head. He insisted we finish the round and, to our great relief, seemed okay.

Later, toward the end of the round, something happened that I found amusing and significant. Robert hit his drive, the ball struck a tree and then ricocheted into the fairway.

"Must be my lucky day," he said.

I couldn't help thinking, I sure hope a lucky day for me never includes getting whacked in the head with a golf ball. He'd already put the event out of his mind, however, and had gotten on with his day.

His perspective is worth adopting and well illustrates how attitude can make all the difference. Events and circumstances, by how we react to them, become a big deal or no big deal at all. The mind determines which, and in turn sets the course for success and happiness or failure and misery.

LEADERSHIP PRINCIPLE: If you don't believe every day is your lucky day, just try missing one.

TAKE CHARGE WHERE YOU CAN

Just the other day, while filling my gas tank at the local service station, I noticed they had something new. Right there on the screen where the pay options appeared was a new option. I understand what it means when it asks if you want to pay with cash, credit card or debit. What I didn't understand was the new "equity" option. So, I pressed the button. When it said, "Please enter mortgage account number," I understood thoroughly.

I'm pulling your leg just a bit, but not much. Fact is, I never thought I'd see the day our monetary standard would shift from the dollar to the price of a barrel of oil. But, I guess stranger things have happened, and might yet.

The control of these things, though, is pretty much out of your hands and mine. But, there are other things of much greater value over which we do have control. Perhaps we should concern ourselves more with these matters and less with the others.

William Jennings Bryan said, "We spend relatively too much time in the perfecting of the things which man uses and too little time in the perfecting of man himself." I realize that sounds like a rather simplistic approach to coping with money disappearing from our pockets. I also know it sounds rather philosophic. Coming from Bryan it is. For me, it makes for good Barber-osophy — which is common sense if it is anything at all.

Common sense says we ought to give the most thought and energy to what really matters, and to what we can really do something about. For instance, we can do something every day about our attitudes. Over that, we have control. Mind you, sometimes my wife Sherry lets me know I don't have a very firm grip on my attitude, but that doesn't change what could and should happen between our ears. However, far too often, the media, co-workers, customers or family members determine for us how we think and how we view life. If they tended to our other business as often as they tend to this, we might tell them MYOB. When it comes to attitude, however, we generally don't mind at all. Then we wonder why our attitude is not better.

As far as outward circumstances, I'm inclined to agree with Dwight D. Eisenhower: "Things are more like they are now than they ever were before." Life is life and people are people, with a few new wrinkles (for both) in each generation. Yet, regardless of such, it is nonetheless true: "The last of the human freedoms is to choose one's attitude in any given set of circumstances." (Victor Frankl). The challenge is to exercise that freedom by cultivating the right thoughts, rather than by letting others do our thinking for us, while bestowing on us their perspectives and attitudes.

Thinking for ourselves! Ah, yes, there's the rub. Thinking is so inseparably connected to attitude.

Not many of us can take the approach of Laurel and Hardy. They had no bad thoughts. But, the fact is, they had no thoughts at all. We, on the other hand, live in the real world of thoughts — good and bad.

What are we doing to control them? To perfect the man himself? To exercise our true human freedom?

May I suggest that we surround ourselves as much as possible with positive, upbeat people? That we read good books and listen to good speakers, in person, and on CD? That we spend less time in front of the TV, and more time in worthwhile endeavors?

In time, you'll begin to notice that fewer things make a difference to you, as more things make a positive difference in you.

LEADERSHIP PRINCIPLE: Take control of the one thing over which you can exercise the most control.

THE TURN-UP-THE-RADIO APPROACH

Have you ever owned a car that rattled? It's not a problem that's always easily solved — unless you have a good radio. Then, if you turn the volume up high enough, it drowns out the rattle and you tend to forget about it.

Lots of things in life tend to fit that pattern. We make the necessary adjustments, and get used to the problem.

In politics the adjustment might involve masking problems with rhetoric. In other areas, the adjustment involves finding a suitable distraction, or convincing ourselves we're too busy to deal with the issue — or, that it's really not that important anyway. This holds true in our homes, our careers and even our personal development.

As an illustration of this principle, in 1993, when J.B. sold me the barbershop, the deal included 60-year-old barber chairs (that continue to increase in value), animal heads, a 1951 model Admiral television set, gigantic steer horns and memorabilia of all sorts. I also became the owner of some unusual waiting chairs.

For comfort, the chairs were hard to beat. They were also great conversation pieces, because customers sometimes had a hard time figuring out where they came from. We often explained that they were once dryer chairs in a beauty shop, and that we had simply taken the dryers off.

Not long after I bought the shop, Sherry and I took the chairs in the parking lot, hosed them down, did minor repairs and proudly placed them back in our shop. Over the years, we've watched as children played, parents chatted and customers read— while seated in those chairs.

Over the same time, the padding in some chairs wore out and on others the upholstery began to tear. No big deal. Much like turning up the volume on the car radio, I would just sit in a chair where the padding was still tolerable, and cover the tears by placing the newspaper over them. Problem solved!

Actually nothing was solved, because neglect never solves anything. It only continues to manifest itself in other seemingly insignificant ways, like with rotten planters for our outside flowers and faded lettering on the windows.

As with other types of businesses, these oversights were not the result of something that was premeditated or planned. They had just been allowed to slide, through loss of focus. After all, I also have a speaking business to think about.

However, what we tend to grow used to because of day-to-day exposure, customers see from a different perspective. They see it as indifference and a lack of enthusiasm. From another point of view, even though people who work in and are part of the business grow used to gradual deterioration, they nonetheless show greater enthusiasm when things are fixed up and spruced up.

So, at J.B.'s Barber Shop new planters with beautiful new flowers, new lettering on the windows, new red striped chair cloths, and new leather waiting chairs (compliments of Sherry, The Barber-osophet), created a whole new outlook for customers and barbers.

LEADERSHIP PRINCIPLE: Neglect in our attitude, our appearance or our environment is seldom deliberate, sudden—or excusable.

JOB #1—HOW WE MAKE OTHERS FEEL

About twenty years ago, when our married daughters were in elementary school, they had a bicycle accident. Jo Ellen, our oldest, lost control of her bike and ran into her sister, Amanda, who was standing right in her path. Suddenly the front fender of the bike slid between Amanda's fingers, and left a sizable gash that required several stitches.

The thing I remember most about the incident took place after we returned from the doctor. Amanda stood in our den, held up her bandaged fingers and, with absolute innocence and candor, declared, "Now I finally have something important to talk about!"

What a commentary on people— young and old. We all want to feel important and to have something important to tell others.

As children, we couldn't wait to tell others how we got our bruise, our cut or our broken bone. As adults we're sometimes the same with illnesses and surgeries. They make us feel special. They become badges of honor.

We act somewhat like a friend I had who broke his neck and, though he healed, subsequently referenced everything to before or after his accident. We, too, are prone to hang on to such personally important events. We need to feel important.

The various ways in which this need is met are rather significant. In fact, knowing how a person gets that feeling of importance tells us a great deal about the person. I heard of a mother who, at a Little League ballpark, told her son, "I do everything else for you. You're going to play baseball for me." In this case, her sense of importance was wrapped up in her child. It makes you wonder how she will fill the void when the child grows up.

Other illustrations could be given, but the point remains the same. However, in addition to the obvious point regarding man's need to feel important, there are two additional observations to be made: (1) The greatest difference in successful and unsuccessful people, those who have things figured out and those who never "get it," is in how they get their feeling of importance. (2) Successful people are usually those who satisfy the other person's need to feel important.

The second of these observations came to mind when Sherry came home one day from the doctor. We had changed doctors and started going to a gentleman who, along with his family, has been coming to J.B.'s Barber Shop for many years.

Though the switch was solely on my judgment, and I kind of stuck my neck out, Sherry was tremendously impressed following her routine visit. In fact, she couldn't stop talking about the experience. She talked about how he asked her this and that, and checked for this and that. He ran such and such a test. He was very thorough.

As she talked non-stop, one thing came to my mind. In her entire adult life, he is probably the very first doctor who ever really made her feel important, and like her health (which is very good) was job #1 with him and his staff.

She was tremendously impressed! Not once did she mention, though, how impressed she was with where he studied medicine, how long he had been in practice, how his office was decorated or how conveniently located it is — all of which are impressive. All such paled in significance when compared to the fact that he made her feel special.

LEADERSHIP PRINCIPLE: In business, and all relationships, nothing matters more than making the other person feel important.

PUT HIGH TOUCH INTO HIGH TECH

"If you scream at me one more time this deal is off!"

So went the punch line to the story a customer told me about one of his employees.

The employee kept getting e-mails, regarding a business deal, that were all in caps. The sender didn't realize what upper case letters indicated.

While I don't recall ever sending someone an e-mail that was all in caps, I'm certain I've sent out my share of dumb messages. After all, Sherry says she pulled me kicking and screaming into the computer age. Now I'm the proud owner of three computers (desktop, laptop and palm) and have three different opportunities for demonstrating computer illiteracy. But, I continue to learn.

By reading, listening and simple trial and error, I've discovered some things that work and things that don't work in e-mails. These things can affect our effectiveness and our credibility as leaders.

1. Give careful thought to the subject line. Weird or mysterious subjects often denote junk mail. Thus, professionals who do not recognize the sender likely just delete the message without finding out if it is legitimate.

The best approach is generally to clearly and concisely state the nature of the message.

If a mutual acquaintance has suggested you contact the person, by all means, say so on the subject line. That way you get the addressee's attention. Quite often I put in the subject line something like, "from Terry L. Sumerlin – Julie suggested I contact you." It generally gets a good response.

2. Be careful about forwards. I'll try to exercise restraint in how much I say on this matter. Truth is, businesspeople are

busy. Most get enough business e-mail that they don't have time for or interest in cartoons, cute stories or unsubstantiated reports. If you think you have something another might be interested in reading, it might be a good idea to call that person or to send a message asking if he would like to receive the article in a forward.

If the person wants to receive it, send it to him or her without including the e-mail address as part of a carbon copy that includes your entire address book. "Blind carbon" is a wonderful, professional option when sending the same e-mail to several at the same time. It protects each person's privacy.

3. Use the addressee's name several times. E-mails can often seem cold and hard.

They can be softened considerably by using the person's name. Depending on to whom you are writing, and the reason, this is not always necessary. Nor should we feel we have to begin every sentence with the person's name. That's annoying even in conversation. But, when mentioned two or three times in most messages, the name is part of a high touch approach.

4. Expect a response when the person gets to it. When we depended on snail mail, we were more patient with the responses. Now, if the response isn't immediate, we want to fire off another e-mail. Effective leaders don't generally do that. They exercise patience, and thus wait a reasonable length of time before sending a follow up message.

5. Never tell someone off in an e-mail. Once you hit "send" you can never unsay it. I know this from personal experience. It's a bitter lesson. Avoid telling anyone off if at all possible. Avoid telling anyone off in an e-mail like you would avoid a rattlesnake. Like the rattler, it will come back to bite you.

LEADERSHIP PRINCIPLE: Whatever form of communication is used, leaders learn the best ways to use it.

TO GET THE BEST EXPECT IT

It was an exceptionally busy time at the shop. I had been off a week, and was paying for it. As part of the catch-up process, I headed across the street to the bank to make a deposit. I also needed to get change for the shop.

It was all really no big deal, and seemed to go smoothly. I chatted with various tellers, as I filled out my deposit slip, and then stepped up to the window. While the teller handled my transaction, she said that she had read my first book and wanted to get the other two.

I promised her that I would get them to her, completed my business and left with the books on my mind.

Later, as I was driving home, a question went off in my head: What did I do with the bank bag full of change? I had also intended to deposit the change. In no time I realized I had left it sitting on the counter where I had filled out my deposit slip.

It only contained about $50 but, nonetheless, it was there for the taking.

Immediately, I got on my cell phone and called the teller who had handled my transaction. As I explained the situation, she said, "Sure, I see the bag is still there where you left it." She then very kindly agreed to deposit the change into my account.

The next day I went back in the bank with the books I had promised the lady, and in order to pick up the money bag from her. We both commented on how amazing it was that the bag had not been taken, and how it restores one's faith in people.

Yet, in my mind, there is something that says even more than the money bag regarding the good in people. It is the fact the in over 54 years of receiving checks at J.B.'s Barber Shop we have been disappointed only twice. I realize that we are located in an exceptional community. I also appreciate the fact that we serve third and fourth generation customers. But, that said, 54 years and two bad checks?

For that reason, it is with a great deal of satisfaction we tell folks, "Yes, we take checks."

It says they are our loyal customers and that we trust them. It is also my way of opposing the signs we encounter every day that read: "Sorry, no checks accepted," "No bills larger than $20 accepted," and "Please prepay."

Every time I'm asked to prepay for gas, I'm tempted to ask the cashier if he or she can give me a deposit on my deposit. How do I to know the cashier won't run out with my money while I'm pumping gas? Why should the cashier be so worthy of my trust when I'm not worthy of hers? In view of such, I find it very satisfying to give my business to those I know and trust and who likewise trust me.

Yet, I realize we don't have much choice when the shoe is on the other foot. In other words, we don't generally screen our customers. So, let me hasten to say I'm not advocating lack of caution or a foolhardy approach in business transactions.

On the other hand, our point does involve a general principle of effective human relations that has been around a very long time.

LEADERSHIP PRINCIPLE: When we expect the best of people, that's usually what we get.

LONG LASTING LEADERSHIP

Statistically, fewer people die over the age of a hundred than any other age. Lest we jump to the conclusion that if we live to that age we've got it made, consider another statistic. One hundred percent of those who live past a hundred will die — eventually. In the words of singer Hank Williams, "I'll never get out of this world alive."

Few things have brought this truth home to Sherry and me more than when, several years ago, we were preparing for a European cruise. I suddenly realized we had not made preparation for the unthinkable, were it to happen in the air or at sea. We had no will and had given no instructions to our children regarding any of our wishes. So, before departure, we had wills drawn up and gave all our vital information to our kids.

Though all this might sound morbid, and you might wonder what it has to do with leadership, it is all very relevant. You see, until influence is seen as something that will outlive us and that will be of lasting value to others long after we're gone, we are perhaps merely self-serving manipulators rather than leaders.

When our son, Jon, went into the Air Force, I told him that I expected him to become a better man than his dad. And, I hope he will influence his son to be better than his dad. In my mind, this is the kind of leadership that makes the world a better place, by making a real difference in people's lives. Many are the stories of such leadership.

One such story involves a longtime customer of J.B.'s Barber Shop. He modestly told me of the difference he and his wife are making with a young lady. She was waiting tables in a restaurant they frequented in a small town. They began to visit with her, and they learned of her college plans. Ultimately, they were so impressed with her character and ambition that they are now funding her entire college education. I was deeply touched by his story.

Though you also may appreciate his story, you might be thinking, "I'd like to do that, too, if I could afford it." Believe it not, I said essentially the same thing to my wife: "Someday I want us to be able to do the same thing."

But, what about now? How can you and I make a significant difference right now?

What if, when Sherry and I find that young student who is going to school and waiting tables, we leave an extra $20 on his table? What if we also habitually request his section and then inquire with sincere interest as to how his classes are going, as well as give a word of encouragement from time to time? You think it could make a difference?

Another way in which we can make a lasting difference is with our time. Benjamin Franklin said, "Dost thou love life? Then do not squander time, for that the stuff life is made of."

Those who truly love life not only do not waste time, they invest it in others. That way their character, their expertise and their wisdom continues on for years to come. This kind of leadership can take place with our children, students, athletes, followers or those we choose to mentor. But, it takes a consistent commitment of time.

Very few of us will ever be remembered by virtue of having a building or prominent structure that bears our name. Perhaps we can nonetheless be inspired by one of the world's greatest architects.

In London is one of Christopher Wren's greatest creations. It is St. Paul's Cathedral, rebuilt by Wren after the Great Fire. He is buried in the church crypt, which bears a huge blue plaque in his honor. The plaque bears the following words: "Reader, if you seek his memorial, look all around you."

LEADERSHIP PRINCIPLE: If it won't outlast us, it's pretty shallow leadership.

BEWARE THE MOOD MUGGERS

One of the most famous phrases of the United States Declaration of Independence is "life, liberty, and the pursuit of happiness." I'm not totally convinced that, with such a phrase, our founding fathers did us any favors.

It seems many of us are about to run ourselves to death in pursuit of happiness. From entertainment to travel to food to thrills to things to even substance abuse, many run faster and faster chasing after happiness and become more frustrated and more unhappy in the process.

Like the fleeting butterfly to a child, happiness seems just beyond our grasp. Could it be that we have misconceptions regarding happiness? Could it be that happiness is not a thing, a situation or a place, but rather a state of mind resulting from purpose and fulfillment?

The "pursuit thing" can cause us to lose our perspective in life regarding things that really matter, and thus can leave us empty and unhappy. Other erroneous thought patterns can do the same thing.

Before we look at a few of these misconceptions, permit me to touch on how happiness relates to leadership and team building. Generally speaking, a good attitude broadens and enhances these scopes of influence. Though Abraham Lincoln and others might be cited as examples of effective leaders who were given to melancholia, they were effective in spite of such. Not because of it.

This is not to say giddiness enhances leadership. It doesn't. Yet, a positive, upbeat attitude does. So, let's consider a few patterns of thought that, like a constant "pursuit of happiness," might make us unhappy rather than happy.

One of these attitudes involves a failure to live in the moment. This reminds me of a story involving my maternal grandparents. Sunday lunch was always a treat at their house. It is one of my favorite childhood memories. One Sunday, as we were eating wonderful lemon meringue pie that my grandma had made for desert, someone commented, "Grandma, this is sure good pie." Without a moment's hesitation, she replied, "Yeah, but it would be better if it was coconut."

After that, whenever my mother and I wanted a good chuckle, all that was necessary was for one of us to mention this incident. But, it was usually mentioned in a context of needless discontent.

It has often caused me to wonder why, if things are good or okay now, I destroy the moment by wishing for something else? Why do I become preoccupied with yesterday's problems or with tomorrow's uncertainties? Put another way, why can't each of us just live in the moments which are perfectly fine? We would be amazed at how much happier such an approach would make us.

Another thief of happiness is the you-make-me-happy (unhappy) approach. This is where one is totally dependent on the actions or attitudes of others for personal happiness.

With parents, this takes the form of being only as happy as your least happy child. For families, we have the familiar line, "If mama ain't happy, ain't nobody happy." A customer once told me a corollary to this: "If daddy ain't happy, nobody cares." Yet, in spite of the intended humor in both statements, they point out a major flaw in happiness as it relates to relationships: that it depends on others. It does not.

Happiness is a state of mind, and we can control our minds. While others often contribute to a good attitude, they take such from us only through our consent.

Closely related to this, is a third area of consideration. This says that we cannot be happy until circumstances are to our liking. A customer recently indicated this with reference to the economy. He tried to draw me into a negative conversation while I was cutting his hair. As kindly as I knew how, I commented to him that I did my part when I voted, and that now I choose not to worry about things I can't do anything about.

"I can do something about it!" he nearly shouted.

"What might that be?" I quietly asked.

"I can protest!"

I indicated that we have that right, but at some point, we have to just go on with our lives. The gentleman did not seem to get my point. I trust you do.

Someone has said, "Worry is like rocking in a chair. It gives you something to do, but it doesn't get you anywhere." When we can do something constructive — great! Worry, on the other hand, steals happiness.

LEADERSHIP PRINCIPLE: Spend less time pursuing happiness and more time guarding against negative influences.

A CHICAGO HAIRY CARRY

It all seemed so simple. Sherry and I flew to Europe and back about a month prior without a single hitch. So, what could be easier than flying to Chicago for a speech to the local chapter of Help Desk International? Up one day and back the next.

Little did I know how hairy carriage by plane and taxi could be. The flight was "direct," by way of Houston and Birmingham. As scheduled, it left at 1:30 p.m., and all seemed to go well.

As we approached Houston, though, the pilot came over the intercom. "We've been informed that Hobby Airport has been closed due to thunderstorms. We've been circling a while and because we are running low on fuel, we're going back to San Antonio for refueling." We spent about 30 minutes on the ground there before starting over.

On the second try, the airport was open. After boarding new passengers at Hobby, we finally headed for Birmingham. Feeling a bit better about the situation, I wrapped my travel pillow around my neck, settled back in the seat and was out like a light.

When the announcement was made concerning our approach to Birmingham, I opened my eyes to find that the ladies across the aisle, along with a flight attendant, were looking at me. I wondered if I was drooling.

One of the ladies said, "We've been talking about you. Aren't you going to Chicago?"

When I said yes, the flight attendant said, "I'm sorry, but we just got word this plane is going back to San Antonio. We'll have to put you on a flight to Louisville, then Chicago."

Great! Things were not looking good.

As if that were not discouraging enough, one of the ladies in the group pulled out a road map, unfolded it and began a rather intense search. Could she be our navigator?

When I finally arrived in Chicago at 11:00 p.m., I felt like the hippie the guy found in his closet. When asked what he was doing in there, he replied, "Like, man, you gotta be somewhere."

I was glad to finally be somewhere, and especially glad that "somewhere" was where I was supposed to be. The only problem was the hotel and meeting place were still an hour away.

Fortunately, the only luggage I had was carry-on. I didn't have to find anything but a cab.

No problem. For a mere $122 he could get me there. Late night, unfamiliar setting. Options were rather limited. So off we went.

After about an hour, and at midnight, I suddenly felt the cab go across the shoulder grid that's designed to awaken a driver. A few minutes later, the cabbie pulled over to the shoulder and we came to a stop.

"You don't mind if I take a few minutes for a nap, do you?"

You've got to be kidding, I thought.

In an attempt to keep us moving in the direction of the hotel, I decided to get out of the back seat, into the front, and talk to the driver to keep him awake. It seemed like the least I could do for a mere $122.

Though it's far too late to make a long story short, a summary of the return flight is that once again Houston storms caused problems. My flight arrived in San Antonio at 2 a.m. instead of 10:45 p.m.

I absolutely love to speak, and generally like traveling. I jokingly commented to Sherry, though, that the glamour had worn off speaking just a tad.

LEADERSHIP PRINCIPLE: Expect some days to be more challenging than others.

NICE NEVER HURTS

No big vacation this year. Sherry and I made that decision before the summer started.

Since trips to the Dallas and Tampa areas are planned to welcome our third and fourth grandchildren into the world, we decided vacations would be limited to Sherry traveling with me on speaking engagements.

The first stop was the Gaylord Texan Resort in Grapevine, Texas. I'd always heard things are big in Texas, but in there this Texan was wide-eyed. What a place! An atrium with four and a half acres of greenery, and as if that's not enough, there's a mini San Antonio Riverwalk. And, then, there are the shops and restaurants.

As an added dimension of the trip, we traveled round-trip by Amtrak.

The dining, scenery and reading time proved well worth the time it took to get there and back.

After a morning presentation to the Texas Association of Community College Business Officers, I had an opportunity to sort of hang out while Sherry rested in our room. Ultimately I wound up in the Java Coast with book in hand, and took a seat in front of the TV to wait for the start of game two of the UT vs. LSU College World Series finals.

Suddenly, a gentleman stood beside me to also watch ESPN. "I'm waiting for the CWS," I commented.

"Did you see that game last night?" he excitedly asked.

We chatted a bit and I mentioned that I really wanted to watch the upcoming game on the 52-foot screen in the nearby lounge, but the room was reserved for a social. He said he was part of that group and was surprised I couldn't get in.

"I'll be right back," he said, and away he went.

In a few minutes, he came back and handed me an unclaimed name badge from his medical conference. "Tonight you're Sue," he said. "Help yourself to all the food." I didn't but thought what he did was very funny and unbelievably thoughtful.

Keep that story in mind, please, as I relate one more incident that occurred the same evening in the same coffee shop.

I had phoned up to the room to see if Sherry had finished resting and if she would like to meet me in the coffee shop. She suggested we call it a day and have coffee in our room.

I thought, I'll surprise her with a blueberry muffin to go with our coffee. So, I stepped over to the counter to place my order.

As the young lady behind the counter got my muffin, we chatted and I mentioned we would make coffee in our room. She smiled and handed me two of their coffee cups.

"That coffee in the room is not very good," she said. "Try it, but feel free to come back down and get ours."

Theirs was $3.50 a cup. How nice was that? I had already paid her for the muffin, but reached back in my pocket for a tip.

"No," she said.

When I persisted she said, "I did that because you actually treated me like a person instead of just seeing someone who takes orders and works a computer."

I was stunned, and assured her I had enjoyed talking to her and others should as well.

Two stories — one point. But what is it?

Is it that I'm such a fine person everyone wants to do me favors? Not at all. I have times when I'm a jerk. And, Sherry gently lets me know when she observes that in me because she sincerely wants me to always be a good person.

The point is simply this: Good people habitually give others what they want most of all — respect, attention and a feeling of importance. Though we may not always be rewarded in turn, when it does happen, it's generally because nice usually produces nice.

LEADERSHIP PRINCIPLE: Nice and leadership are not exclusive concepts, but rather go hand in hand.

THE CURE FOR BELLYACHING

A meeting planner with the Dallas Independent School District, in a recent pre-presentation interview, told me she had been greatly touched by the following story and that I just had to include it somewhere in my presentation. Perhaps, it will mean as much to you.

It was a quiet Thursday morning at the barbershop. J.B was in the shop reading the paper and I was seated at the desk in the office, talking on the phone.

Suddenly, the front door opened and someone asked, "Is Terry here?" Quickly I ended my conversation, and opened the office door to see who had come in. I was pleased to see one of my regulars, a very successful businessman that I especially like.

He said that his wife and son were outside in the car, and he wanted to know if I would mind taking a look at his 16-year-old to see if there was something I thought I could do with his hair. I asked if he thought it would work best if I came outside or if he would like to bring him inside. In a moment, with the help of his wife, he brought his son in.

As I walked over to the door to greet his wife, and the boy whose hair I had cut since he was just a little tyke, my heart sank to the floor. I thought I had mentally prepared myself, but I was totally unprepared for what I saw.

Several months prior, the dad had come in for a haircut. As usual, I asked, "Joe, how are you?"

"Not too good today," he solemnly replied. "Billy is in Brooke Army Medical Center with second and third degree burns over 60 percent of his body." (For privacy, the names are fictitious.) He went on to explain that Billy had an accident while driving the classic pickup the two of them had restored, and the truck had caught fire.

The boy that was standing in the door of my barbershop had just spent his first night at home, after spending several months in BAMC's burn unit. Had I not known his parents and the circumstances, I would have never recognized him. As you might expect, the strain still showed on his parents' faces.

As I carefully cut his hair, avoiding the skin grafts and tender spots on his head, I thought of those days when the sweet mom who was holding his head would bring her little boy in for his after-school haircut. Her life, her son's and her husband's would never be the same. Such a beautiful family. It was all such a dirty, rotten, sorry, no-good shame!

On the more positive side, these events remind me of another little boy and of his great uncle. The uncle owned a dump truck and would occasionally take the nephew with him on various runs. It was a great time, as we would go bouncing off down the road.

Just before my Uncle Archie died, due to the effects of diabetes, Mom and he had an amusing conversation in the hospital. There is certainly nothing funny about diabetes, but it didn't keep Uncle Archie from having a great sense of humor.

Sadly, he had both legs amputated in order to save his life. In an effort to brighten his day, when Mom walked in his room, she cheerfully asked, "Well, how you doing today, Uncle Archie?"

With a gleam in his eye, he smiled and said, "Well, I can't kick."

Bless his heart, literally, I guess he couldn't. But, if anyone ever had anything to kick about he certainly did.

Though Uncle Archie passed many years ago, I'm very happy to report that Billy is doing very well and has gotten on with his life. They both remind us of a truth that is very important to leadership and success.

LEADERSHIP PRINCIPLE: We don't have to look far to realize that most of us really have so very little to kick about most of the time.

HURRY UP AND DEVELOP SOME PATIENCE

My dentist/customer told me that popcorn is bad for my teeth. When I asked why, he said that most people can't stop eating it after the popped kernels are gone. So, they're apt to crack a tooth on the unpopped portion.

Well, at night Sherry and I love popcorn and T.V. But, we're careful not to eat the unpopped kernels. We're also careful about how long the popcorn stays in the microwave. Two minutes, forty-five seconds is all it takes. Not a lot of patience is required.

In the winter, if we want hot tea, we stick two mugs of water in the microwave, set the timer for two minutes, take it out when the timer goes off, spoon in the tea and sweetener and we're set. It doesn't take long at all.

Then if we decide to text someone, the reply is often in a matter of minutes — or less.

Unfortunately, life is not as instantaneous as popcorn, hot tea and text messages. So, patience is often required.

Ah, but there's the rub!

Patience, at least for me, is a tough one. I'm like the guy that prays, "Lord, give me patience — and hurry." But I've learned that however impatient I have been, it has rarely made the situation better. It likely won't change much for you, either.

Following are some techniques, though, that might change our attitude.

The first technique is one I learned from Sherry. When I become frustrated because meeting planners don't get back with a phone call or e-mail as quickly as I think they should, she says: "I just don't understand it. Surely they're just sitting around with nothing to do but get back to you." Point taken.

Yet, I sometimes have to be reminded (and perhaps you as well) that people are busy and that I'm not the only person on earth.

A second approach often used in sales involves doing what we can to shorten the decision making process that can often drag on and on. Sometimes it helps speed the decision along if we ask two vital questions: 1) Who else besides you will be involved in the decision and 2) what information will he/she need in the decision making process?

With others in our lives, by clearly stating the rewards or consequences, we can often speed up the decision.

A third technique was suggested to me recently by a customer. He has a case that is being considered by the United States Supreme Court. That would cause a fellow to get a bit antsy, wouldn't it? He has avoided this by taking some time off and vacationing with his family, and by involving himself in other aspects of his law practice. Though he is eager to get a response, he isn't anxious or impatient because his mind is otherwise occupied.

One additional tip for handling impatience and anxiety is something I ran across several years ago. As a result of what I read, I taped a small sign in bold red letters on my computer monitor. It simply says: "NEXT."

Whatever we are waiting on, there is always something or someone else out there that deserves our attention. In sales, "next" can be taken a step farther. It then becomes — SW, SW, SW, SW. That stands for: Some will, some won't, so what, someone's waiting. NEXT!

We have all heard that with age comes maturity. However, sometimes age comes alone and leaves patience behind. On the other hand, mature people of any age have developed patience.

LEADERSHIP PRINCIPLE: Develop a reasonable degree of patience with circumstances and with people.

WHAT TO DO WHEN YOU'RE WRONG

One day an old-timer, who was born in San Antonio and had never lived anywhere else, was in the barbershop. The conversation involved Austin, and I was shocked by what the old gentleman had to say.

Keep in mind that Austin is about 75 miles straight up I-35 North. Occasionally it can be driven in about an hour. There are times, however, because of heavy traffic it might take closer to three days.

Anyway, when the old-timer heard the reference to Austin his only comment was, "You know, one of the days I need to get up there. I've heard that's a real nice place."

He'd lived 80-something years in San Antonio and had never been to Austin! My guess is he didn't get out much. However, recently I felt like I was that old gentleman.

The situation involved one of the things I like to do in connection with speaking — acting. Several years ago I took acting lessons, which I think greatly improved the entertainment value of my presentations. It also equipped me to do auditions for television commercials and industry training videos.

So, I went to Austin to audition for a Farm Bureau Insurance commercial. The trip up there and the audition seemed to go well. Nothing unusual occurred. I played the part of a preacher conducting a wedding ceremony. Piece of cake!

When I finished the audition and headed home, that's when the problem occurred. I decided to take a different route back to I-35. How difficult could that be?

The highway runs right through the middle of Austin. Couldn't miss it if I tried.

Wrong!

With my mind still on the audition, and with a change in my route, I wound up on the wrong highway. Then I had to figure out how to correct my mistake. So, I exited, turned around and headed back the other way — only to get on another wrong highway. This time, in order to turn around, I decided to take a shortcut and follow the tracks of the illegal cars that had driven across the median. Breaking the law was not exactly consistent with the role of the preacher I'd just played in the audition.

Suddenly, with cars whizzing past me on both sides of the median, I'm joined by a motorcycle cop with lights flashing and siren blaring. The thought crossed my mind that perhaps I'd done something really stupid.

"Good afternoon, sir," he said. "I've stopped you because you are illegally crossing a median. May I see your license and proof of insurance?"

"Yes, sir," I said as I reached for my wallet. "I'm so sorry, officer. I have been downtown and am trying to get back on I-35, but I have taken the wrong highway twice. I'm hopelessly lost and totally confused."

"Where are you going?" he asked.

When I told him I was headed home to San Antonio, he responded very kindly by telling me how to get to I-35. He also told me something that helped keep the cost of the material for this story to merely time and fuel.

"Normally, I would write you a ticket. But, since you're from out of town, and obviously lost, I'm not going to do that." Then in order to get me off the median, he said, "There's a break in the traffic now. You'd better hurry."

I breathed a sigh of relief and thought about what I'd learned. Obviously, I'd re-learned that it's always best to avoid illegal or stupid activities. But, there is also a leadership principle in this.

LEADERSHIP PRINCIPLE: When you're wrong and you know you're wrong and the whole world knows you're wrong—admit it quickly and emphatically.

TREATMENT FOR AN ALL TOO COMMON AILMENT

I had a customer in my barber chair and one waiting. The one waiting has served in a number of governmental positions, has served several presidents and was once our ambassador to Great Britain. He had returned just that morning from a very important trip to Israel.

The customer in my chair asked the former ambassador a loaded political question. With great diplomacy, he proceeded to answer and was met with strong disagreement by the fellow in my chair. In short order, the inquirer firmly ended the conversation with, "I don't want to talk about it."

I was speechless, which was a good thing since I was not part of the conversation to begin with. Also, it would probably not have been a good thing for me to tell my customer I thought his conduct was just about the greatest display of prejudice and rudeness I had ever witnessed.

After all, had he not asked the man's opinion? Whether he agreed or disagreed was beside the point and fell into the who cares category.

No doubt the customer's emotions and biases had clouded his sense of reason and common courtesy. Yet, lest you and I think we are immune to such attitudes and actions, I hasten to ask, "How open-minded are we?"

Though the symptoms might vary from individual to individual, to some degree we are all afflicted with the same mental disease of prejudice. Some prejudices, of course, are harmless. Yet, others can significantly affect our lives and our livelihood. Thus, let's think for a bit about the concept of open-mindedness.

How receptive are we to new ideas? William James said, "A great many people think they are thinking when they are merely rearranging their prejudices." Does that describe you or me? Just because we never considered something or never even heard of such, doesn't make it wrong, impossible or a bad idea. Nor, for that matter, is an old idea wrong because it's old.

Let's face it. No one wishes to be so open-minded his brains fall out. On the other hand, it's no great honor to have a concrete mind. That's the kind that's all mixed up and permanently set. Al Smith, former governor of New York, often replied to critics by saying, "Let's examine the facts." When it comes to new ideas, you would expect nothing less from any fair, open-minded individual.

In close connection with the preceding, the unbiased are also open to reasonable, valid change within organizations. As previously noted, Peter Shane said, "If you advocate change, you will have to understand that there is no change so small that it threatens no one."

Because we feel threatened when it comes to change, we often close our minds. When pushed hard enough, we feel angry and resentful. Consider, however, that there are some changes that are better for the business and the customers. Taken from the follower's perspective, however, leaders need to carefully consider the dynamics of change and act with great wisdom.

As we should be open to new ideas and to change in organizations, we should also be unbiased with respect to areas in our lives and careers that require self-improvement—change. It's so easy to take an emotional approach here: "I'm doing the best I can. That's just the way I am. You just don't understand me."

Objectively considered, how are your relationships? How are your evaluations? How mature are your attitudes? Do you find everyone in the world out of step but you? Perhaps some changes are in order.

If a person wants to be prejudiced about certain foods, sports teams or even his grandkids, such is relatively harmless. But, if prejudice keeps us from being better people, or causes us to mistreat others, we ultimately wind up hurting ourselves and lessening our influence as leaders.

LEADERSHIP PRINCIPLE: Beware of that disease of weak minds known as prejudice.

TIPS FOR FLICKING OFF THE ASHES OF LIFE

As I was doing a phone interview for a presentation in the Dallas area, the gentleman concluded the conversation with a friendly question. "How was your trip to Italy?"

I answered in the same way I've answered everyone for the past two weeks. "I'm probably the only person you know who, on Saturday, April 17th, flew to Atlanta and back just for lunch."

I then went on to explain that because of volcanic ash my flight to Rome was cancelled and I was sent from Atlanta back to San Antonio.

As you might expect, it was very disappointing. Though the trip and my speaking engagements with a church and the U.S. Navy in Sicily will be rescheduled for this fall, the let down from months of preparation and anticipation was enormous.

A close friend put it all in perspective, though, when he sent me a text that said, "Well, look at it this way. There's some Barber-osophy in there somewhere." So, here it is:

First of all, some things simply are what they are. Good leaders realize when such is the case, you just pick up the pieces and go on. If flights weren't going to Europe, they weren't going to Europe. And, all of the screaming, yelling, whining and bellyaching in the world weren't going to change things except to make them worse. And, herein is a second point.

People who are not responsible for a problem can just do so much to solve it. The Delta agent in Atlanta was incredibly helpful. She was also very caring. "Oh, my, that's awful about your speaking engagements." That said, she was then very conscientious about making arrangements for me to get back home as soon as possible. If, on the other hand, I had verbally abused her over something she could not control she might have taken a different approach.

A good friend who is general manager of two large hotels told me of a situation he heard of where a lady at an airport check-in counter was trying to help a passenger who was being verbally abusive. Finally she said, "Sir, as best I can tell there are only two people in this entire terminal who care about your problem and one of them is rapidly losing interest."

It never helps to abuse those who weren't the cause of a problem to start with and are only trying to solve it.

A third lesson from this incident, in addition to that of acceptance and patience, has to do with a sense of humor. All the rest of that day I received text messages from my friend who had made reference to Barber-osophy lessons. The messages were all designed to make me laugh. He knew I was disappointed.

Finally, I texted him back with a simple message: "Shut up." I was just kidding—sort of. He was just trying to do the same sort of thing I've done with the "lunch in Atlanta" line. Simply trying to lighten what otherwise was a downer day.

Disappointing things happen. No one has special exemption status. However, people with positive attitudes and influence approach these things in a positive way.

LEADERSHIP PRINCIPLE: Accept what must be accepted, respect those who are seeking a solution—and then just laugh.

HOW TO COPE WITH DISCOURAGEMENT

Have you ever been discouraged? Have you ever known an effective leader that you thought might be discouraged?

Perhaps because good leaders don't generally share their personal problems with their followers, we sometimes think they never get discouraged. Not true.

Everyone gets down from time to time. This is evidenced by the question asked by Chick-fil-A founder, S.Truett Cathy: "How do you identify someone who needs encouragement?" His answer, "That person is breathing."

Stated conversely, every living, breathing person occasionally gets discouraged. And, we get discouraged for similar reasons.

We get down about personal finances, the economy, failure, rejection, family struggles, careers, relationships, health concerns or a myriad of other issues.

During these times, an encouraging word often helps. But, one may or may not receive that word of encouragement. What else can help during these low periods?

Many find pen and paper of great help during such times. Writing down all that is troubling one can be of great benefit.

Though imagination can often work for us, when we're discouraged it generally doesn't work to our good at all. Rather, it tends to magnify existing issues and breed new ones. However, when issues are in black and white, this is less likely to happen. And, seen in concrete form, worries often become less daunting.

Another tool for handling discouragement is to do something constructive. Personally, I've found that rather than remaining discouraged on those occasions when a speaking engagement I really want doesn't happen, the best thing I can do is get on the phone and find a new client

Whatever it might be that has us discouraged, the key is to not sit around waiting for circumstances to change. If possible, do something to change them. But, regardless, don't just sit and brood.

In close connection with doing something is doing something with others. Discouragement tends to cause brooding which in turn hatches isolation. Big mistake.

People are sources of encouragement and opportunity. We can receive neither if we withdraw. Nor can others make us laugh, give us new ideas or inspire us if we avoid them. In good times and bad, people are invaluable assets.

We must remember, however, that people are not to be used simply as whine bottles (i.e. to be used only for whines). Though friends can be good listeners during times of discouragement, they can also be a means of continuing to pour the whine, while prolonging our discouragement and making more of the situation than it really is.

And then, something we tend to forget in dealing with discouragement: "This too shall pass." Life and moods tend to cycle. What is a really big deal today may not be so big tomorrow, days from now or a year from now.

We've all heard that without valleys there would be no mountains, or that all sunshine makes a desert. Though trite expressions, both are nonetheless true. They also illustrate a principle that can help us respond appropriately to discouragement. That principle is that we can't have the exhilarating, enjoyable times in life without having some of the other times.

LEADERSHIP PRINCIPLE: Learn to handle discouragement as a temporary inconvenience rather than a permanent condition.

THE PERSON YOU REALLY ARE

I never listen to talk radio and, even if I did, I would not be foolish enough to call with a comment. No matter what you say, or how valid your argument, the host always has the last word.

So, I surprised myself this morning when I called the listener line to one of San Antonio's country stations – KJ 97. Actually, I rarely listen to radio at all since I prefer CDs; and, as I've said, "call in" is certainly not my thing. But, this morning I couldn't resist.

After I punched the button on the radio, I immediately heard them talking about the Tony Parker incident at the airport. Apparently, he and an airport employee had a verbal altercation when he refused her request for an autograph. It seems he was in a hurry to catch his flight.

The DJs made comments in defense of the popular Spurs player and then, between songs, took comments from listeners. That's when something came to mind that I felt compelled to share.

In a voice that I could easily envy, the DJ took my call: "Good morning this is KJ 97."

"Yes, I'd just like to comment on the Tony Parker matter. I don't know Tony personally, so all I know about him is just what I've read. So, I have no comment regarding him. However, I do know former Spurs player, Steve Kerr, and I would just like to say that I don't believe you would ever hear of such an incident involving him."

Before he moved, Steve was a customer at the barbershop. So, we became acquainted. I went on to tell the radio host: "He pulled up behind me one day at the car wash and recognized me as being in the car in front of him. He immediately got out of his car and came to my window to say "hi."

The radio personality thought it was a nice story, and thanked me for sharing it. "But you have to admit," he said, "that Steve Kerr was not the star Tony Parker is. That kind of status brings lots of demands."

"That's true," I replied. "But, even if Steve Kerr were a megastar, I don't believe it would change who he basically is as a person. Do you?" He seemed to agree.

I'm not famous. But, I hope that were I to ever be famous I would be like my friend, Steve Kerr, or like a very famous professional speaker I know.

At the very pinnacle of his career, he did an event in Austin. I had just begun my speaking career and planned to go hear my mentor (through his books and CDs). So, I wrote him with a request. I wanted to spend a few minutes with him before or after his Austin speech to tell him how he had changed my life.

In a few days I received a phone call from his longtime executive assistant, Laurie Magers. She said Zig Ziglar had received my letter and wanted me to pick him up at the airport so that we might have a few minutes to visit on the way to the hotel.

I was totally blown away. Zig Ziglar, internationally famous motivational speaker and bestselling author, wanted to meet with me, someone he didn't even know? I still get a lump in my throat just thinking about it.

Some years later, Texas Monthly, did a feature article on him. The author asked the question, "Is he for real?" Or, is he too positive and too good to be true? They concluded what I did. No doubt he's for real!

I found out first hand that he practiced what he preached: "People don't care how much you know until they know how much you care." For our purposes I would change this just a bit:

LEADERSHIP PRINCIPLE: Mature people don't care how GOOD you are until they know how good YOU are.

GO FOR THE GOLD

The preteen "cleaned up" nicely and looked good with his new haircut. In fact, I was plumb proud of my work. But, he was totally under-whelmed. In an attempt to get a smile, I said, "You really don't need to be quite so excited about this haircut." His mom laughed, but he didn't.

After they left, another customer commented to the effect that the boy would likely have been happier about his haircut had it been his idea. "Probably so," I replied. "But, apparently that was the golden rule in action. Mom had the gold. So she made the rule."

After we enjoyed a laugh, I began to think more seriously regarding the real meaning of the golden rule. No question, in dealing with others, its value is as gold. Yet, few seem to really understand it, and even fewer apply it.

I pointed these things out yesterday morning when I gave a brief chapel talk at Florida College, a religiously oriented liberal arts college that I attended 41 years ago near Tampa in Temple Terrace, Florida.

Last night I was privileged to kick off their annual Enrichment Series with a presentation on leadership. Both were exciting occasions for me.

In the chapel talk, I connected the two presentations by saying "effective leadership is positive influence – the golden rule at its best." Then I discussed for a few minutes what the golden rule is and isn't and how it would tie into my evening presentation. Following are a few things I pointed out.

Both the religious and non-religious have heard it: "Do unto others as you would have others do unto you." Actually that's a paraphrase of Jesus' words.

For certain, the principle involves something better than returning meanness for meanness, rudeness for rudeness or injury for injury. Yet, we somehow tend to feel justified in personal or business relationships when we mistreat those who have mistreated us. In response to such, we might simply ask, "How's that working for you?"

Your response might be, "It sure doesn't work as well as when I am nice to others." Indeed! Yet, in light of such we sometimes misconstrue the rule to mean that we should simply repay kindness with kindness. And, that's certainly an improvement over rude for rude. However, it doesn't require much of us. Most can be nice to those who are nice to them.

"Well," one says, "I think I apply the golden rule by being a completely harmless person. I wouldn't deliberately hurt anyone." That's great! The world certainly has room for a lot more harmless folks.

But, the golden rule is proactive. It's not what we don't do. It's what we do. And what we do, if we apply the rule, is treat others as we would like to be treated – without regard for what another has done to us or for us, and without regard for future repayment.

Tough to apply? You bet! In fact, oftentimes my failure in applying the rule disappoints me. But, we must keep trying, because the benefits are well worth the effort. Though it's a rare person who truly understands the rule and consistently applies it in every relationship, that individual is generally rich in friendships, relationships, health and happiness.

LEADERSHIP PRINCIPLE: Enrich your life by going for the gold in all relationships.

Other Books by Terry Sumerlin

Available at www.barber-osophy.com:

Barber-osophy: Shear Success for Your Cutting Edge

Barber-osophy: Hair We Go Again!

A Human Becoming: A Life Changing Voyage

www.ingramcontent.com/pod-product-compliance
Lightning Source LLC
LaVergne TN
LVHW011233080426
835509LV00005B/476